INTRODUCING
ISSUES WITH
OPPOSING
VIEWPOINTS®

# The Middle East

Lauri S. Friedman, *Book Editor*

Christine Nasso, *Publisher*
Elizabeth Des Chenes, *Managing Editor*

**GREENHAVEN PRESS**
*An imprint of Thomson Gale, a part of The Thomson Corporation*

THOMSON

GALE

Detroit • New York • San Francisco • New Haven, Conn. • Waterville, Maine • London

| LIBRARY OF CONGRESS CATALOGING-IN-PUBLICATION DATA |
| --- |
| The Middle East / Lauri S. Friedman, book editor<br>    p. cm. — (Introducing issues with opposing viewpoints)<br>  Includes bibliographical references and index.<br>  ISBN-13: 978-0-7377-3575-8 (hardcover)<br>  1. Middle East—Politics and government—1945——Juvenile literature. 2. Conflict management—Middle East—Juvenile literature. 3. Peace-building—Middle East—Juvenile literature. I. Friedman, Lauri S.<br>  DS63.1.M484215 2007<br>  956.04—dc22<br><br>                         2007003662 |

ISBN-10: 0-7377-3575-9
Printed in the United States of America

# Contents

# Foreword

Indulging in a wide spectrum of ideas, beliefs, and perspectives is a critical cornerstone of democracy. After all, it is often debates over differences of opinion, such as whether to legalize abortion, how to treat prisoners, or when to enact the death penalty, that shape our society and drive it forward. Such diversity of thought is frequently regarded as the hallmark of a healthy and civilized culture. As the Reverend Clifford Schutjer of the First Congregational Church in Mansfield, Ohio, declared in a 2001 sermon, "Surrounding oneself with only like-minded people, restricting what we listen to or read only to what we find agreeable is irresponsible. Refusing to entertain doubts once we make up our minds is a subtle but deadly form of arrogance." With this advice in mind, Introducing Issues with Opposing Viewpoints books aim to open readers' minds to the critically divergent views that comprise our world's most important debates.

Introducing Issues with Opposing Viewpoints simplifies for students the enormous and often overwhelming mass of material now available via print and electronic media. Collected in every volume is an array of opinions that captures the essence of a particular controversy or topic. Introducing Issues with Opposing Viewpoints books embody the spirit of nineteenth-century journalist Charles A. Dana's axiom: "Fight for your opinions, but do not believe that they contain the whole truth, or the only truth." Absorbing such contrasting opinions teaches students to analyze the strength of an argument and compare it to its opposition. From this process readers can inform and strengthen their own opinions, or be exposed to new information that will change their minds. Introducing Issues with Opposing Viewpoints is a mosaic of different voices. The authors are statesmen, pundits, academics, journalists, corporations, and ordinary people who have felt compelled to share their experiences and ideas in a public forum. Their words have been collected from newspapers, journals, books, speeches, interviews, and the Internet, the fastest growing body of opinionated material in the world.

Introducing Issues with Opposing Viewpoints shares many of the well-known features of its critically acclaimed parent series, Opposing Viewpoints. The articles are presented in a pro/con format, allowing readers to absorb divergent perspectives side by side. Active reading questions preface each viewpoint, requiring the student to approach the material thoughtfully and carefully. Useful charts, graphs, and cartoons supplement each article. A thorough introduction provides readers with crucial background on an issue. An annotated bibliography points the reader toward articles, books, and Web sites that contain additional information on the topic. An appendix of organizations to contact contains a wide variety of charities, nonprofit organizations, political groups, and private enterprises that each hold a position on the issue at hand. Finally, a comprehensive index allows readers to locate content quickly and efficiently.

Introducing Issues with Opposing Viewpoints is also significantly different from Opposing Viewpoints. As the series title implies, its presentation will help introduce students to the concept of opposing viewpoints, and learn to use this material to aid in critical writing and debate. The series' four-color, accessible format makes the books attractive and inviting to readers of all levels. In addition, each viewpoint has been carefully edited to maximize a reader's understanding of the content. Short but thorough viewpoints capture the essence of an argument. A substantial, thought-provoking essay question placed at the end of each viewpoint asks the student to further investigate the issues raised in the viewpoint, compare and contrast two authors' arguments, or consider how one might go about forming an opinion on the topic at hand. Each viewpoint contains sidebars that include at-a-glance information and handy statistics. A Facts About section located in the back of the book further supplies students with relevant facts and figures.

Following in the tradition of the Opposing Viewpoints series, Greenhaven Press continues to provide readers with invaluable exposure to the controversial issues that shape our world. As John Stuart Mill once wrote: "The only way in which a human being can make some approach to knowing the whole of a subject is by hearing what can be said about it by persons of every variety of opinion and studying all modes in which it can be looked at by every character of mind. No wise man ever acquired his wisdom in any mode but this." It is to this principle that Introducing Issues with Opposing Viewpoints books are dedicated.

# Introduction

*Say: 'O Peoples of the Book! Come to common terms,' so that we can build peace in the land of peace, the land of Palestine.*

—former Palestinian leader Yasir Arafat

Because they all worship the same God, Islamic tradition refers to Jews, Christians, and Muslims as the three Peoples of the Book. These traditions revere similar texts, share many of the same prophets, and embrace similar outlooks on life, death, and judgment. In the modern Middle East, however, the Peoples of the Book have endured a family feud unlike any other. Their similarities have been overtaken by a frustrating and heart-wrenching conflict that has dominated their lives for hundreds of years, but especially in the twentieth and twenty-first centuries. On any given day newspapers are filled with stories about violence perpetuated by all parties against each other and sometimes amid themselves.

Infused with historical and religious significance, the Middle East provides one of the most dramatic stages for conflict and tension in the entire world. Sacred sites of all three faiths are often crowded into the same areas. For example, the last remaining wall of the holy Jewish Temple, the site of Jesus's crucifixion, and the rock upon which the prophet Muhammad ascended to heaven are found just a few miles from one another. Around these treasures, violent conflict is waged continuously and ferociously. In April 2002, for example, Israeli tanks battled Palestinian gunmen holed up in the Church of the Nativity, the birthplace of Jesus. Similarly, religious militants have taken hostage the holy city of Mecca, where the Islamic religion originally flourished in the seventh century. Iraq, considered to be the historic location of the Garden of Eden, is another ongoing focal point of war and death, especially since the U.S. invasion in 2003. The power and emotion of violent conflict is naturally overwhelming, but these layers of history and religion make the clashes in the Middle East additionally fascinating and dramatic.

It is difficult for outsiders to comprehend what it is like to live in a place where hostility and death may puncture any given day. Middle Easterners have had to construct their existence around such conflict, attempting regular acts amid the most irregular circumstances. A family traveling a short distance to see relatives, for example, may be delayed for hours by checkpoints and intrusive searches. Likewise, fighter jets screaming through the sky might overshadow an afternoon at a park or a beach, constantly reminding people of the state of conflict in which they live. More devastatingly, a simple ride on a downtown bus targeted by a suicide bomber may end in horror, or worshipping at a mosque for Friday prayers can result in rioting and bloodshed.

This reality has caused a sense of fatalism to descend upon Middle Easterners. As conflicts drag on across decades, their lives become enshrouded in hopelessness. People come to accept that conflict is unavoidable and simply absorb violence as a fact of their lives. One Lebanese man put this sense of inescapable despair in the following way: "There is a test we used to do in class to see how easily living things can adapt. You put a frog in a pail of water and gradually turn up the heat. The frog just keeps adjusting to the new temperature until it finally boils to death, because it is so used to adjusting that it doesn't think to jump out of the pail. I feel like that frog."

While enduring this seemingly intolerable violence, however, many have kept a flame of hope alight. Like plants straining to grow through rubble, the people of the Middle East go on with their lives, opening businesses, spending time with their families, and savoring moments of happiness. Their perseverance in the face of so much pain is endlessly touching. Indeed, in the throes of conflict are some of the brightest examples of humanity on earth. These are the people who struggle to make peace with their neighbors at all costs, to live alongside their fellow People of the Book and to make more of their commonalities than their differences. One such visionary was the late Israeli prime minister Yitzhak Rabin, who once said,

> We have come from a people, a home, a family, that has not known a single year—not a single month—in which mothers have not wept for their sons. . . . We say to you today in a loud and clear voice: Enough of blood and tears. . . . We, like you, are

people who want to build a home, to plant a tree, to love, live side by side with you—in dignity, in empathy, as human beings, as free men. We are today giving peace a chance and again saying to you: Let us pray that a day will come when we will say, enough, farewell to arms.

Achieving peace in the Middle East is one of many issues explored in *Introducing Issues with Opposing Viewpoints: The Middle East.* Readers will learn about the key sources of conflict in the region, what viable options exist for conflict resolution, and what role the United States should play in this volatile but rich area of the world.

# Chapter 1

# What Causes Conflict in the Middle East?

*Signs of warfare are a constant presence throughout the Middle East.*

# Israeli Terrorism Causes Conflict in the Middle East

### Chas W. Freeman Jr.

*"As long as such Israeli violence against Palestinians continues, it is utterly unrealistic to expect that Palestinians will stand down from violent resistance and retaliation."*

In the following viewpoint author Chas W. Freeman Jr. argues that Israeli violence against Palestinians fuels conflict in the Middle East and around the world. He argues that Israel illegally occupies Palestinian lands, and thus subjects Palestinians to constant violence and oppression. Furthermore, Israel makes decisions about the peace process unilaterally, meaning it does not consult with the Palestinians about their wishes for their land. Freeman argues it is unreasonable to ask Palestinians to renounce violence against Israel when Israel continues to conduct a campaign of violence against Palestinians. Israel's continued occupation of Palestinian territory is a source of anger and frustration for oppressed peoples all around the world, he concludes.

Freeman is president of the Middle East Policy Council, a nonprofit organization

Chas W. Freeman Jr., "Remarks to the 14th Annual US-Arab Policymakers Conference," The National Council on US-Arab Relations, September 12, 2005. Reproduced by permission.

founded to expand public discussion and understanding of issues affecting U.S. policy in the Middle East.

**AS YOU READ, CONSIDER THE FOLLOWING QUESTIONS:**
1. According to Freeman, what state do Palestinians in the Gaza Strip live under?
2. What does the word "dispossession" mean in the context of the viewpoint?
3. Name five countries experiencing terrorism that the author claims is inspired by Israeli violence against Palestinians.

Once again, I have been honored by the National Council on US–Arab Relations and stand before you to offer a few thoughts on where we—Americans and Arabs—are and where we may go from here. I speak for myself alone, not for any organization with which I am affiliated. I speak because I believe US-Arab relations matter greatly to my country and because, unlike many in Washington, I do not believe in diplomacy-free foreign policy and have a healthy regard for what is now derided as "reality-based analysis."

## The State of Affairs in the Middle East
Some things are, of course, going right in the Middle East. The Saudis are clearly winning their struggle against violent extremists. Palestinians in Gaza have been released from direct occupation by Israeli settlers and soldiers. Lebanese are exploring a new measure of autonomy, following the long-overdue Syrian withdrawal from their country. Syrians, relieved of the burden of keeping order in Lebanon, may finally attempt their own reforms. Women are being admitted to a larger role in society in some Gulf Arab countries. Annoying as the results are to many, the expanded press freedoms pioneered in Qatar continue to spread throughout the region. Experiments with elections as a means of selecting leaders continue to occur. High oil prices have produced an economic boom in many Arab countries, though not, of course, in all.

But, with few exceptions, despite the propensity of the spindoctors here in DC to claim credit for anything positive that happens in the

Middle East, these developments owe little to the state of US–Arab relations and have little impact one way or the other on American relations with the Islamic world. . . .

The Anglo-American occupation of Iraq has come to have much in common with the Israeli occupation of Palestinian lands. In Iraq, as in Palestine, ending the occupation is the prerequisite for reversing the growth of terrorism and restoring peace.

## Israeli Occupation of Arab Lands

Not long ago, many Arabs took obvious pleasure in seeing a few thousand Israeli settlers in Gaza suffer the same sense of powerlessness and dispossession that hundreds of thousands of Palestinians have experienced over the years. It is all too easy to forget that the Israeli withdrawal was unilaterally imposed by the Israeli military on Israelis and Palestinians alike. It was not agreed with the Palestinians as part of a peace process and it has no clear implications for any other part of the occupied territories. It seems likely, in fact, that the people of Gaza

*Israeli approaches to the peace process have played a role in violent reprisals by Palestinians.*

have exchanged occupation by Israeli colonists and soldiers not for freedom but for a state of siege, in which their access to the outside world will continue to be controlled and perhaps severely restricted by their Israeli neighbors. Meanwhile, [former Israeli prime minister Ariel] Sharon, having driven off on his own road, has made it clear that he has no intention of pulling the road map out of the glove compartment and using it to navigate. He gives every evidence of a firm intention to continue to impose rather than negotiate changes in Israel's relationship with its Palestinian captives.

The fact is, of course, that Israeli occupation and settlement of Arab lands is inherently violent. Occupations are acts of violence. The dispossession of people from their land is an act of violence. Preventing people from coming to and going from their own country is an act of violence. And as long as such Israeli violence against Palestinians continues, it is utterly unrealistic to expect that Palestinians will stand down from violent resistance and retaliation against Israelis. Mr. Sharon is far from a stupid man; he understands this. So, when he sets the complete absence of Palestinian violence as a precondition for implementing the road map or any other negotiating process, he is deliberately setting a precondition he knows can never be met.

## U.S. Support of Israel Enflames Tensions

As long as the United States continues unconditionally to provide the subsidies and political protection that make the Israeli occupation and the high-handed and self-defeating policies it engenders possible, there is little, if any, reason to hope that anything resembling the former peace process can be resurrected. Originally intended to provide a basis for trading land for peace, the occupation has itself become the problem. As long as it continues, neither Palestinians nor Israelis will have personal security. As long as it continues, Israel will not find the acceptance by its Arab neighbors that was offered at Beirut in 2002. Moreover, the violent confrontation could at any moment, as it did in the past, spread its murder and mayhem well beyond the region. The most immediate victims of the continuing savagery and injustice in the Holy Land are, of course, Palestinians and Israelis. But their

## Palestinian Opinions About Israel

**Opinion polls of Palestinians reveal they do not believe peace can be achieved with Israel in the near future.**

When asked if they believed peace could be achieved with Israel in the near future:

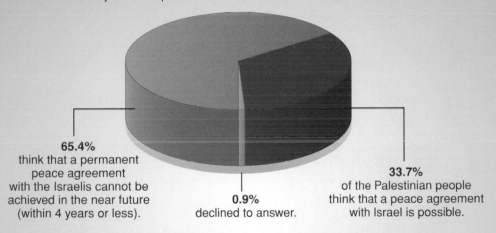

**65.4%**
think that a permanent peace agreement with the Israelis cannot be achieved in the near future (within 4 years or less).

**0.9%**
declined to answer.

**33.7%**
of the Palestinian people think that a peace agreement with Israel is possible.

When asked "Do you believe or not believe that your personal actions can contribute towards reaching a permanent peace agreement between Israel and the Palestinians?"

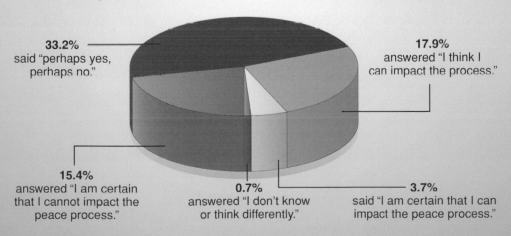

**33.2%**
said "perhaps yes, perhaps no."

**17.9%**
answered "I think I can impact the process."

**15.4%**
answered "I am certain that I cannot impact the peace process."

**0.7%**
answered "I don't know or think differently."

**3.7%**
said "I am certain that I can impact the peace process."

Source: "Views of Peace in the Territories of the Palestinian Authority," Miftah.org, April 10, 2006.

agony disturbs the peace of the world and wounds the hearts of billions beyond their borders.

## Israeli Terrorism Inspires Violence Around the World

The extremism and terrorism bred by the continuing injustices and crimes against humanity in the Holy Land thus continue to take their toll in places as remote from the Holy Land as Britain, Thailand, Nigeria, Indonesia, India, Pakistan, and Afghanistan. In Afghanistan, an American-led military operation to apprehend the perpetrators of 9/11 and to punish those Afghan Salafis who had given them shelter has now taken on a seemingly eternal life of its own. No one can now say when or what might allow the US to disengage from combat against the once discredited but now resurgent Taliban. As in Iraq and Israel, the occupation is becoming the cause of the very problems it was meant to resolve. If one recalls that the objective of al Qa'ida and its extremist ilk has been to drive the United States and the West from the Dar al Islam so that they can seize control of it, the growing antipathy to the American presence is sobering.

**EVALUATING THE AUTHOR'S ARGUMENTS:**

In this viewpoint Freeman explains that Palestinians resort to violence only as a way of retaliating against Israeli occupation of their lands. The author of the following viewpoint, Martin Peretz, calls people such as Freeman "apologists" for Palestinian terrorism. With which author's perspective do you agree? Why?

# Palestinian Terrorism Causes Conflict in the Middle East

## Martin Peretz

*"Terrorism, truth be told, is about the sum total of what the Palestinians have bestowed on our civilization during the last five decades."*

In the following viewpoint author Martin Peretz argues that Palestinian terrorism causes conflict in the Middle East. Peretz explains that Palestinian terror attacks against Israel are unrelenting. They are planned to occur on holy days and target vulnerable segments of the population. Although these attacks are supposed to be an effort to achieve their own nation, Peretz argues that continuing Palestinian violence will inevitably make their dreams of statehood completely unattainable. Peretz further argues that Palestinian attempts to recruit other Arab nations, such as Egypt and Jordan, to their cause has resulted in multiple wars and a constant state of conflict in the region.

Martin Peretz is editor in chief of the *New Republic*, a monthly political magazine from which this viewpoint was taken.

Martin Peretz, "Immature," *The New Republic*, January 20, 2003. Copyright 2003 by The New Republic, Inc. Reproduced by permission of *The New Republic*.

**AS YOU READ, CONSIDER THE FOLLOWING QUESTIONS:**
1. What does the word "apologists" mean in the context of the viewpoint?
2. What do Palestinians hope to gain by attacking poor neighborhoods in Israel, in Peretz's opinion?
3. How does Palestinian terrorism implicate other Arab nations, according to the author?

[F]ormer secretary of state] Warren Christopher wrote last week in *The New York Times* of terrorist attacks "wreaking havoc in far-flung places such as Indonesia, Kenya, Jordan and Yemen." Maybe I am being myopic, but why didn't he mention Israel in that list, the state that suffers most from this savagery? Certainly Bill Clinton's secretary of state wouldn't be the first prominent American to believe that terror against Israelis is different, not quite so satanic, as terror against other civilians. Palestinian terror, say its apologists, is political—the illegitimate means to a legitimate end, statehood. But many peoples have pursued statehood in modern history, and only the Palestinians have pursued it so barbarically. Terrorism, truth be told, is about the sum total of what the Palestinians have bestowed on our civilization during the last five decades.

## Palestinians Delight in Attacking Israel

The Palestinians aren't skittish about claiming this peculiar gift to the world as their own. Take the double suicide bombing near the old bus station in south Tel Aviv this past Sunday evening [in January 2003]. Before all the shattered bodies had been dispatched to hospitals, Islamic Jihad had taken credit for the deed. And, not long after, came word from Hamas that it, too, should share in the kudos. Then, this competition became snarled. The Al Aqsa Martyrs Brigade, an armed gang of Yasir Arafat's own Fatah, announced that, no, it had committed the act. And, then, Arafat's Palestinian Authority (P.A.), itself dominated by Fatah, condemned it. The P.A. boldly promised to act against those responsible. But by now this is an old trick, which only the European Union still seems to believe. The purveyors of murder and the denouncers of murder are the same people. (To make the P.A.'s horror even less credible, authoritative Israeli observers now believe that it was Tanzim, another of Fatah's militias that actually shed the blood.)

This was not the first time these particular Tel Aviv streets had hosted Palestinian carnage. On Tisha B'Av last summer, a day of fasting and mourning for the destruction of the First and Second Temples, terror took the lives of five and wounded dozens over the same pavement. There was another bloodletting earlier. This is a poor neighborhood, and many of those present in its alleys and open spaces are foreign workers, the poorest of the poor.

## Palestinian Terrorism Hurts Their Chance at Statehood

A wise Jerusalem friend speculated that the murderers now target foreign workers because they are the ones on whom Israel depends for the work once done by Palestinians from the territories. The Palestinian aim is to make the Filipinos and Romanians, Nigerians and

*Protests and terrorist attacks by Palestinians fuel discord with Israel and may undermine their goal of attaining statehood.*

Colombians, Turks and Thai, so scared that they leave. If my friend has divined an intention of the Palestinians, it is a mad intention. The intifada has not only brought current agony to nascent Palestine; it has guaranteed that economic misery will continue far into the future. In the coming months, a wall, urged upon Israel by many of its foolish doves and many of its foolish hawks, separating much of the disputed territories from the Israel-to-be, will be an established fact. When (and if) there is a peace agreement, the borders will not again be open for hundreds of thousands of Palestinian workers to share in the prosperity that will surely return to Israel. The peril of admitting an alien and hating workforce is simply too great. Edmund Burke wrote in his *Letters on a Regicide Peace* (1796), "War never leaves where it found a nation. It is never to be entered upon without mature deliberation." At what might have been the dawn of a real state, the Palestinians started this macabre war in a fit of delirium. The war has been and will remain, long past the day when agreed rules govern relations between Israel and whatever becomes Palestine, a calamity for their people.

## Dragging the Arab World into the Conflict

One index of the immaturity of Palestine even as a concept is that its elites still turn to neighboring Arab countries to fight their battles for them. (The term "Palestinians" is immature as well. The U.N. Partition Plan of 1947 never called the local Arabs "Palestinians" and neither did the crucial 1967 Security Council Resolution 242). When the Egyptians, Jordanians, and Syrians sent armies to fight in 1948, 1967, and 1973, they were there not on behalf of the Palestinians but on behalf of their ambitions for sovereignty over the lands of what was historically called Palestine. The other Arabs talked a lot about Arab Palestine but did little. They are now doing even less. In real terms,

# Palestinian Terrorism Is Unrelenting

Israelis continue to be victims of Palestinian terrorist attacks against buses, marketplaces, homes, restaurants, tourist spots, and other locations.

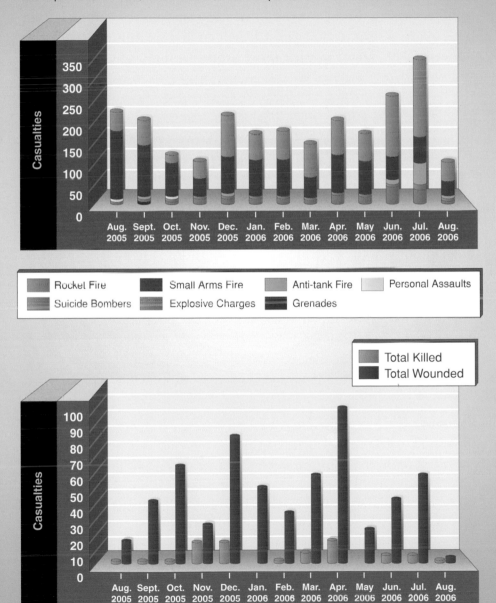

Source: Israeli Ministry of Foreign Affairs, "Victims of Palestinian Violence and Terrorism Since September 2000," September 2006.

the Palestinians are now on their own. . . . Egypt is now in a panic that the deteriorating situation of the Palestinians will inflame Cairo's rent-a-mob populace. So, just as the bombs went off in Tel Aviv, [Egyptian president] Hosni Mubarak was trying to convene meetings with Fatah, Hamas, Islamic Jihad, and two "Marxist" murderous bands (one, the Popular Front for the Liberation of Palestine; the second, the Democratic Front for the Liberation of Palestine) aimed at an agreement to stop terror against Israeli civilians within the armistice lines of 1949. Terror outside those armistice lines, of course, would still be perfectly acceptable.

## EVALUATING THE AUTHOR'S ARGUMENTS:

In this viewpoint Peretz argues that by engaging in terrorism Palestinians hurt their chances for achieving their own country. How do you think the author of the preceding viewpoint, Chas W. Freeman Jr., might respond to this argument? Explain your answer using evidence from the texts.

**Viewpoint**

**3**

# The Need for Oil Causes Conflict in the Middle East

**Kevin Phillips**

*"Everything about Iraq (and neigh- boring Kuwait) gen- erally boil[s] down to oil."*

In the following viewpoint author Kevin Phillips argues that the need for oil has caused conflict in the Middle East. Phillips explores how the quest for oil drew the boundaries of Middle Eastern nations and served as the basis for the Gulf War in 1991 and the ongoing Iraq War. Phillips credits the growing need for oil as the primary reason the United States invaded Iraq. He argues it was unfair of America's leaders to have led the nation into war under the guise of fighting terrorism when the real reason was to have access to the region's rich oil reserves.

Phillips is the author of *American Theocracy: The Perils and Politics of Radical Religion, Oil, and Borrowed Money.* He has also contributed to the journal *American Conservative,* from which this viewpoint was taken.

**AS YOU READ, CONSIDER THE FOLLOWING QUESTIONS:**

1. What does the word "fraud" mean in the context of the view-point?

2. How many extra barrels of oil will the United States need per day by 2010, according to Vice President Dick Cheney?
3. According to the author, what was the first building U.S. forces seized after entering Baghdad in 2003?

Few lies have wound up injuring Americans more—in everything from automobile gas tanks and winter heating bills to diminished U.S. global standing—than a rarely revisited three-year-old fib-fest involving [President] George W. Bush, [Secretary of Defense] Donald Rumsfeld, and [British prime minister] Tony Blair. Since World War I, history is clear: the British and Americans have been pre-occupied with only one thing in Iraq—oil. Yet in 2003, as their troops again disembarked, the pretense was all about good and evil, democracy and freedom. The disastrous outcome of the unacknowledged Middle Eastern mission, the struggle for petroleum, has rarely been discussed.

## Covering up the Aim of the Iraq War

In part, that's because a credulous press has swallowed an extraordinary fraud. Speaking on behalf of George W. Bush, then White House Press Secretary Ari Fleischer insisted in February 2003, "If this had anything to do with oil, the position of the United States would be to lift the sanctions so the oil could flow. This is not about that. This is about saving lives by protecting the American people." In November 2002, Defense Secretary Donald Rumsfeld had likewise declared, "it has nothing to do with oil, literally nothing to do with oil." On the other side of the Atlantic, British Prime Minister Tony Blair told Parliament in early 2003, "Let me deal with the con-

> **FAST FACT**
>
> The Middle East contains over two-thirds of the world's remaining oil reserves and one-third of its remaining gas reserves. It is currently responsible for approximately 30 percent of the daily world oil production, a share likely to rise substantially over the coming decades.

spiracy theory that this has something to do with oil. There is no way whatever that if oil were the issue, it wouldn't be simpler to cut a deal with Saddam Hussein."

Horse manure. In the run-up to war, from Alberta to Texas, oilmen gossiped about the centrality of oil. Meetings of petroleum geologists buzzed about the so-called "peak oil" forecast that a dangerous top in global production was only a decade or two away. Specialized publications guesstimated how much taking over Iraqi oil could mean for profits and Exxon and Chevron. Polls of ordinary citizens from Europe to Latin America and the Mideast produced similar findings: people thought the invasion was about oil.

## The Relationship Between War and Oil

The Gulf War in 1991 certainly had been. When the first President [George H.W.] Bush went into the Persian Gulf in force that year, it was indeed about petroleum. He openly stated, "our jobs, our way of life, our own freedom and the freedom of friendly countries around

*The presence of rich oil fields in the Middle East has been a source of conflict for several decades.*

the world would all suffer if control of the world's great oil reserves fell into the hands of [former Iraqi dictator] Saddam Hussein." The idea that Saddam Hussein was a second Hitler was a rhetorical embellishment. Back during the Cold War, even when Washington worried about the Soviet Union rolling into Iran and reaching the Persian Gulf, American concern arose out of the geopolitics of oil, not some abstract commitment to representative government and democracy.

The British had indulged their own motivational buncombe [nonsense] in the aftermath of the First World War when the Marquess of Curzon, Britain's foreign secretary, said that the influence of oil in the new boundaries drawn for Iraq was "nil." "Oil," he said, "had not the remotest connection with my attitude, or with that of His Majesty's Government, over Mosul." By 1924, as the British agreed to cut American oil companies in for a share of Iraq's oil production, the centrality of oil was obvious. Curzon's claim that London sought to bring freedom and self-government to the Arabs was mocked in Parliament and on Fleet Street.

## "We Will Need Millions of Barrels"

But that was 80 years ago, and today's opinion-molding elites—in the United States, at least—are far more gullible. Too many are still psychologically embedded in the hard-charging pretense that surrounded the 2003 U.S. military incursion. The revelation that Saddam's much trumpeted weapons of mass destruction seem not to have existed has yet to lead to the next logical re-evaluation: just how much more credibility should be given to the three sweeping "it wasn't about oil" assurances quoted earlier? After all, if oil was involved, then the U.S. disaster in Iraq, doubly bungled, represents the greatest wartime failure since James Madison let the British burn Washington in 1814.

Vice President Dick Cheney, the one top official who avoided denying that oil had anything to do with the Iraq invasion, is precisely the

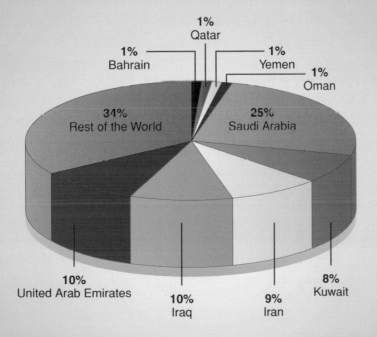

**Oil in the Middle East**

**Together, Middle Eastern nations control 66 percent of the world's oil supply.**

- 1% Qatar
- 1% Bahrain
- 1% Yemen
- 1% Oman
- 34% Rest of the World
- 25% Saudi Arabia
- 10% United Arab Emirates
- 10% Iraq
- 9% Iran
- 8% Kuwait

Source: Public Broadcasting Service, 2006.

man whose attentions must be examined to illustrate the depth of oil motivations. In 1999, when Cheney was still the head of Halliburton, the oil-services giant, he made a shrewd speech to the London Institute of Petroleum in which he gloomed over coming oil-supply problems: "By some estimates, there will be an average of two per cent annual growth in global oil demand over the years ahead along with conservatively a 3 percent natural decline in production from existing reserves. That means by 2010 we will need on the order of an additional 50 million barrels a day."

## Oil Has Always Caused Strife in Iraq

Those barrels would have to come largely from the Middle East, and a few years earlier the *Wall Street Journal* had reported an Anglo-American oil company consensus: that Iraq, specifically, was "the biggie" in terms of potential future reserves. . . .

Prior to the U.S. invasion in 2003, everything about Iraq (and neighboring Kuwait) generally boiled down to oil. Suffice it to say that Iraq's new boundaries were drawn around oil after World War I; Axis forces invaded from Syria in 1941 in pursuit of petroleum; important Persian Gulf surveys generally concentrated on oilfields; the maps Cheney looked at in 2001 were about oil; and on entering Baghdad in 2003, the first government building U.S. troops occupied was the Oil Ministry, with its seismic maps of the rich Iraqi oilfields.

**EVALUATING THE AUTHOR'S ARGUMENTS:**

In this viewpoint Phillips accuses the U.S. government of undertaking the war in Iraq in order to satisfy its need for oil. What pieces of evidence did he provide to support this claim? Did he convince you of his argument? Explain why or why not.

Viewpoint
4

# The Need for Water Causes Conflict in the Middle East

*"There will be no long-term security for any resident of the Middle East without fair distribution and a just solution to the sharing of water resources."*

Isabelle Humphries

In the following viewpoint author Isabelle Humphries discusses how the scarcity of water in the Middle East is a perpetual source of conflict. The region's water sources are not equally divided among Israel, Jordan, Syria, Lebanon, and the Palestinian Territories, she explains. Humphries argues that Israel's desire to control major water sources has resulted in war and other hostilities. The 1967 War, for example, broke out in part because Israel attempted to divert the headwaters of the Jordan River to irrigate its fields and provide drinking water for its people. Until the area's scarce resources are shared equally among the region's residents, Humphries predicts Middle East conflict will continue.

Humphries conducts research on the Palestinian refugee community inside Israel. Her work has been published in journals such as the *Washington Report on Middle East Affairs*, from which this viewpoint was taken.

Isabelle Humphries, "Breaching Borders: The Role of Water in the Middle East Conflict," *Washington Report on Middle East Affairs*, vol. 25, September, 2006, pp. 20–22. Copyright 2006 American Educational Trust. All rights reserved. Reproduced by permission.

**AS YOU READ, CONSIDER THE FOLLOWING QUESTIONS:**
1. What is the conflict between Israel and Lebanon over the Wazzani River, as discussed by the author?
2. What percent of West Bank water is used by Israel, according to Humphries?
3. In how many years does the UN estimate residents of Gaza will lack access to drinking water?

In months when Israel is not pounding the life out of its Lebanese neighbors, a tourist to Israel may hire a car and drive around the beautiful northern regions of former mandate Palestine and Syria. Here one may look around at the stunningly green surroundings, go kayaking in the Jordan River, admire the beautiful waterfalls at ancient Banyas in the Golan, or dip one's feet in the waters of the Sea of the Galilee. Those feeling adventurous may hand over their passports at the gate, enter the Israeli-occupied Alawite village of Ghajar, and look down at the little stream of the Wazzani in the small valley below.

## The Middle East Conflict Is Really About Water

Israel has not ensconced itself in the Golan Heights for mere tourism opportunities, however. The Israeli media machine would have one believe that the country is engaged in a struggle to protect its very existence against imaginary Arab military giants. Yet a trip around the places in which it chooses to maintain its borders is far more revealing of the root of conflict with its Arab neighbors—water. Israel has no plans to make peace with Syria and return the Golan Heights, because by doing so it would give up its control of springs, rivers and the Sea of Galilee [also called Lake Tiberias]. Nor will it hand over any significant West Bank land to Palestinians, for in doing so Israel would have to abandon lush aquifers (underground water reserves), key access to the Dead Sea, the Jordan River, and surrounding fertile plains.

Division and distribution of a static resource such as land is difficult enough, but problems are magnified when the resource is able to flow across international boundaries. Take the Israeli furor over Lebanon's installation of new pumping facilities on the Wazzani River in the fall of 2002. Despite the fact that the activity took place entirely on Lebanese

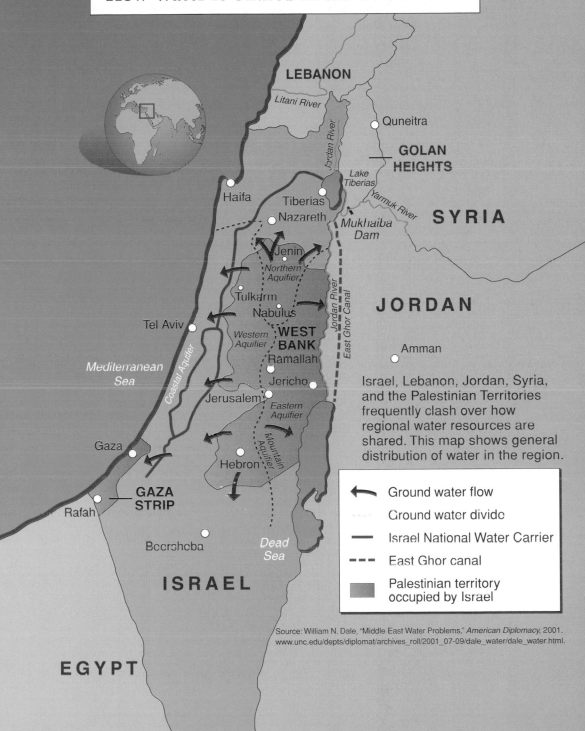

# How Water Is Shared in the Middle East

LEBANON

*Litani River*

Quneitra

GOLAN
HEIGHTS

*Jordan River*

Lake
Tiberias

*Yarmuk River*

SYRIA

Haifa

Tiberias
Nazareth

*Mukhaiba
Dam*

Jenin

*Northern
Aquifier*

Tulkarm

*Jordan River*

*East Ghor Canal*

JORDAN

Nabulus

Tel Aviv

*Western
Aquifier*

WEST
BANK

Amman

*Mediterranean
Sea*

*Coastal Aquifier*

Ramallah

Jericho

Jerusalem

*Eastern
Aquifier*

Israel, Lebanon, Jordan, Syria,
and the Palestinian Territories
frequently clash over how
regional water resources are
shared. This map shows general
distribution of water in the region.

Gaza

Hebron

*Mountain
Aquifier*

GAZA
STRIP

Rafah

Beersheba

*Dead
Sea*

ISRAEL

←    Ground water flow

    Ground water divide

───   Israel National Water Carrier

- - -   East Ghor canal

    Palestinian territory
occupied by Israel

Source: William N. Dale, "Middle East Water Problems," *American Diplomacy*, 2001.
www.unc.edu/depts/diplomat/archives_roll/2001_07-09/dale_water/dale_water.html.

EGYPT

land, Israel raised a ruckus because the Wazzani is a key tributary of the Hasbani River. And although the Hasbani flows for 25 miles inside Lebanon, it crosses into the Israeli-occupied Syrian Golan, feeding into the Banias and Dan Rivers, which in turn flow into the Jordan—ultimately providing water to the rapidly reducing Sea of Galilee, Israel's largest source of fresh water.

While Beirut stated that it was Lebanon's internationally recognized right to pump Wazzani waters for surrounding low-income Shi'i villages, Israel objected, claiming, as usual, that the "terrorist" entities of Syria and Hezbollah were behind the development plan. Lebanon retorted by pointing out that, even after pump installation, it would be taking only 10 million cubic meters annually—while Israel, on the other hand, uses some 150 million cubic meters a year from the Wazzani and Hasbani.

## Water a Factor in the 1967 War

That particular episode of the water conflict did not erupt into full-scale war, but at other times water has provided the trigger. In his memoirs, [former Israeli prime minister] Ariel Sharon claimed that the 1967 war (resulting in Israeli occupation of the Golan and prevention of Syrian access to the Sea of Galilee) was launched as an unavoidable response to Syrian attempts three years earlier to divert the headwaters of the Jordan.

An analysis of historical evidence, however, provides a very different story of the events leading to the 1967 war. It was Israel, in fact, which first made moves to divert the headwaters, provoking an international crisis, yet convincing many that Syria was the aggressor. Israeli historian Avi Shlaim dates Israel's first attempt to divert the Jordan River to as early as 1953, when Syria responded not by attacking the Jewish state, but complaining to the U.N., which eventually put a halt to the Israeli plan the following year. Ten years later, however,

Israel began to pump water from the Sea of Galilee into its National Water Carrier—a grave threat to vital Syrian, Lebanese and Jordanian water sources. It was in response to this Israeli move that Syria planned to divert Jordan water into its own territory.

Remaining in control of the Golan Heights today allows Israel to irrigate settlements as far as the Negev desert through its National Water Carrier pipeline. The diversion of waters to this artificial carrier has grave implications, resulting in the depletion and salinization of the Jordan River south of the Sea of Galilee, and devastating agriculture on the Jordanian side of the river. The Jordanian government's diversion of the Yarmuk cannot adequately compensate for this loss.

## Water a Source of Israeli-Palestinian Conflict

Israeli control of water is as much of a concern for Palestinians as it is for Arab neighbors. Whether for the few Palestinian farmers remaining inside the Israeli state, or those in the West Bank and Gaza, Israeli water policy is directed at destroying any remaining Palestinian agriculture. The million Palestinians inside Israel are primarily a flexible

*Scarcity and unequal distribution of water throughout the region have led to clashes.*

manual labor force for Jewish industry, as are—when curfews allow—1967 Palestinians. Even where Palestinians remain in control of small pieces of land, Israeli water policy usually sees to it that there is not enough water to grow crops.

Situated above the mountain aquifer, central West Bank towns such as Qalqilya and Nablus have traditionally exported crops across the Middle East. Yet today, despite the availability of sophisticated technology, Israeli policy means that many Palestinians do not have enough water even for themselves, let alone to irrigate the few fields that have not yet been confiscated.

Palestinians should have ready access to water from the mountain aquifer (divided into three), the Jordan River basin and the Gazan coastal aquifer. Aquifers are replenished through rainwater seeping through the ground, and water accessible via wells and springs. According to [the Oslo Peace Accords], two West Bank aquifers are to be shared between Israelis and Palestinians, leaving the Gazan coastal and the third West Bank aquifer solely to Palestinians. (Palestinians, of course, have no access to the Sea of Galilee—their share having been taken in 1948). According to Oslo, Syrians, Jordanians, Palestinians and Israelis all have a share in the Jordan River system (although 97 percent of the river passes through areas only occupied by Israel since 1967). Currently Israel has assured that its citizens have the highest per capita water consumption in the entire Middle East—and four times as much as the Palestinians among whom they live.

International law clearly states that Israel should not be taking water from areas occupied in 1967. Yet even if Oslo had been followed to the letter, it assured inequality by giving Israeli water authorities overall control of water resources. Palestinians may not drill for water without Israeli approval, yet Israel can pump as much water as it likes into its illegal settlements. More than 80 percent of West Bank water is taken by Israelis on both sides of the 1967 line. . . .

## A Just Sharing of Resources Will Lead to Peace

In contravention of Oslo, Israel continues to pump from the Gaza coastal aquifer—which, as levels fall dangerously low, draws in salt water from the Mediterranean. Two thirds of water is used for the Israeli agricultural sector, which represents only 3 percent of Israel's annual GDP, while the greater percentage of Palestinian farmers must rely on insufficient sources of rainwater for 90 percent of their agricultural activity. Desperate for water, Gazans also are overpumping this source, as their inadequate sewage networks continue to leak raw sewage into the supply. Medical sources in Gaza note an increase in kidney disease and other dangerous water-related illnesses. The U.N. estimates that in less than 15 years Gazans will not have access to drinkable water. . . .

There will be no long-term security for any resident of the Middle East without fair distribution and a just solution to the sharing of water resources. Without regional cooperation on protecting rapidly depleting resources such as the Jordan River and the Dead Sea, not even Israel can count on secure water forever.

**EVALUATING THE AUTHOR'S ARGUMENTS:**

In the viewpoint you just read, Humphries uses history, statistics, and examples to make her argument that water is a source of conflict in the Middle East. She does not, however, use any quotations to support her point. If you were to rewrite this article and insert quotations, what authorities might you quote from? Where would you place these quotations to bolster the points Humphries makes?

# Sectarian and Ethnic Tensions Cause Conflict in the Middle East

*"If Iraq breaks into three different pieces—the Kurdish north, the Shiite south, and the Sunni mid-section—the result could be disastrous for Iraq's neighbors and for American interests."*

**Sabrina Tavernise**

In the following viewpoint, Sabrina Tavernise documents the rising tensions between Sunnis, Shiites, and Kurds. The groups have a long history of mistrusting each other and now increasingly attack each other as they vie for power and influence. Furthermore, Tavernise warns, ethnic and sectarian tensions in Iraq could spread to create unrest in the entire Middle East. Nine Middle Eastern countries have mixed Sunni and Shiite populations, she explains, and a civil war between Shiites and Sunnis in Iraq could enflame tensions in other nations. The growing ethnic conflict in the Middle East could also have serious repercussions for American interests in the region, she concludes.

Tavernise is a reporter for the *New York Times*. She is based in Baghdad and reports on the Iraq War.

**AS YOU READ, CONSIDER THE FOLLOWING QUESTIONS:**
1. What historical event caused the split between Sunnis and Shiites, as described by the author?
2. What Middle Eastern nations have mixed Sunni and Shiite populations, according to Tavernise?
3. Name three things that Tavernise reports have helped deepen the divide between Iraqi Sunnis and Shiites.

Ammar Abed Khalaf is a 24-year-old university student in Baghdad who wanted to marry his girlfriend. But despite several attempts, he has been rejected by her family because he is a Shiite and she is a Sunni. Abed Khalaf, who lives in a Baghdad neighborhood that has been tormented by sectarian assassinations for more than a year, says he feels more resignation than anger over the rejection. "I do not blame her father or her mother," he says. "It is because of the situation."

Of all the changes that have swept Iraqi society since the U.S.-led invasion three years ago, one of the most critical is the heightening of tensions between Iraq's two main Muslim sects: Sunni and Shiite. Since Iraq was created in 1920, the government had been controlled by the Sunni minority, who make up just 20 percent of the population. Under the dictatorship of Saddam Hussein, the government ruthlessly repressed Shiites—killing as many as 100,000, for example, when they rose up against him in the aftermath of the first Gulf War in 1991. These injustices caused sectarian tensions that were kept in check by the authoritarian nature and brutality of Saddam's regime.

But since Saddam was removed from power in April 2003, the lawless environment and the growing insurgency have encouraged these tensions to surface. They are increasingly evident in the day-to-day lives of Iraqis— like Abed Khalaf's inability to marry his Sunni girlfriend—and in the bombings and executions killing thousands of Iraqis, which appear on the news back in the U.S. every night.

One such incident, the February 22 [2006] bombing of a Shiite shrine in Samarra, set off waves of violent reprisals that have killed hundreds of Iraqis in recent weeks. The violence has gotten so bad that many believe Iraq is teetering on the brink of civil war.

*Conflicts between Shiites and other groups have increased as they vie for power in Iraq.*

## Centuries of Conflict Among Three Groups

Iraq's population of 26 million is divided into three main groups:
About 60 percent are Shiite Arabs, about 20 percent are Sunni Arabs,
and 17 percent are Kurds. (The Kurds, who are concentrated in northern Iraq, are also Sunni Muslims, but they belong to a different ethnic group. Their region, which has been much less affected by the violence, is the most stable part of Iraq today.)

The split between Sunnis and Shiites dates to the seventh century when, according to Muslim tradition, the Prophet Muhammad died, and there was a dispute over who would take over as Islam's leader. The two groups share the basic tenets of Islamic belief. However, over the centuries, Shiites and Sunnis developed distinctly different social, political, and religious practices. The two sects have often viewed each other with suspicion, which has sometimes escalated into violence, such as in the civil war in Lebanon in the 1970s and '80s.

## Deepening Ethnic Divisions

In Iraq today, these distinctions are becoming more and more important. The vast majority of the 12 million voters in Iraq's December elections cast ballots along sectarian and ethnic lines. Meanwhile, social life has withdrawn from restaurants and cafes, where different groups mingled, to homes, largely for reasons of safety.

The effects on Iraqis' personal lives are profound. Mixed marriages are more carefully considered. "For a parent, the first question now is going to be: Sunni or Shiite?" says Shatha al-Quraishi, an Iraqi lawyer who specializes in family law. "People are starting to talk about it. I can feel it. I can touch that something has changed."

Sectarian tensions in private lives are far from universal: Iraqis of different sects have mixed for decades and still do. But anecdotal evidence from interviews with lawyers, court clerks, and social workers suggests that fault lines that have always existed are now becoming more distinct. An analysis provided by one family court in central Baghdad shows that mixed marriages were rare to begin with, making up 3 to 5 percent of all unions in late 2002. But by late 2005 they had virtually stopped.

"For the coming 10 years you can record the biggest changes in the Iraqi community," says Ansam Abayachi, an Iraqi social researcher. "The Sunnis will be on one side, the Shia (Shiites) on the other, and there is no mixed family."

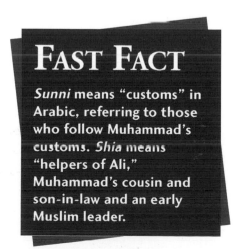

## FAST FACT

*Sunni* means "customs" in Arabic, referring to those who follow Muhammad's customs. *Shia* means "helpers of Ali," Muhammad's cousin and son-in-law and an early Muslim leader.

# Ethnic Breakdowns in Iraq

Shia Arabs, 55%

Kurds, 21% (Sunni, Shia, Yezidi)

Sunni Arabs, 18.5%

Assyrians, Chaldeans, Armenians, 3.5% (Christians)

Turkomans, 2% (Shia and Sunni)

Mandians, 0.5% (Sabaeans)

Sparsely populated

Source: M.R. Izady, Wikipedia.com

## Rising Tensions

After being in control so long, many Sunnis resent their lost power. Feelings have been further inflamed by the systematic killings of Shiites by suicide bombers and assassinations of Sunnis by Shiites, some of them tied to the new Shiite-led government. The violence has driven many families to seek safety by migrating to areas where their religious group predominates, thus reinforcing the sectarian divide. Children come home asking if they are Sunni or Shiite.

In addition to reports of Sunnis no longer allowing their children to marry Shiites and vice versa, one mixed couple even received a series of threatening phone calls demanding that they divorce or be killed. But most cases are more subtle. A counselor at the Center for Psychological Health in Iraq says one of her patients, a Sunni woman, recently received a marriage proposal from a Shiite. One of the woman's aunts forbade the union, saying she would refuse to greet a man she knew to be Shiite.

"We used to dismiss such stances," says Abayachi. "They were old-fashioned. They were not civilized. They were just holding to a tradition that was meaningless."

## An Earthquake for the Middle East

So why is this so important? If these tensions aren't resolved, they could drag Iraq into a civil war—some believe Iraq is already in the midst of one. And that has profound consequences for the 133,000 American troops currently stationed in Iraq, and for the rest of the Middle East. If Iraq breaks into three different pieces—the Kurdish north, the Shiite south, and the Sunni midsection—the result could be disastrous for Iraq's neighbors and for American interests. Experts believe the Sunni region could become a safe haven for terrorist groups like Al Qaeda.

"A civil war in Iraq would be a kind of earthquake affecting the whole Middle East," says Terje Roed-Larsen, the special United Nations envoy for Lebanon. "It would deepen existing cleavages and create new cleavages in a part of the world that is already extremely fragile and extremely dangerous. I'm not predicting this will happen, but it is a plausible worst-case scenario."

In addition to Iraq, eight Middle Eastern countries—Oman, Bahrain, Lebanon, Yemen, Kuwait, Syria, the United Arab Emirates, and Saudi Arabia—have sizable populations of Shiites living side by side with Sunnis, and there is concern in many of them that a split in Iraq could lead to conflict at home.

For Iraqis, the conflicts—many of them deeply personal—have already begun. Fatin Abdel Sattar is a Sunni Muslim from Baghdad who has seen the sectarian tensions divide her own family. Her teenage son has stopped using his Sunni name in Shiite areas of the city. And her sister's marriage fell apart as her Shiite husband turned his anger over old wounds on his Sunni spouse.

"It was like an eruption of a volcano, hidden inside for all those years," Abdel Sattar says of her former brother-in-law. "Those who were oppressed before, they have a weakness inside themselves. They live with this history. They can't get rid of this feeling."

## EVALUATING THE AUTHOR'S ARGUMENTS:

In the viewpoint you just read, Tavernise describes the sectarian tensions that threaten to push Iraq into civil war. Consider the reasons given for the conflict between the two groups. What suggestions would you offer for easing the tension between them? How might the United States be able to help the two groups peacefully coexist? Explain your reasoning.

# Chapter 2

# What Can Bring Peace to the Middle East?

*People around the world show support for the peace process in the Middle East.*

# Democracy Can Bring Peace to the Middle East

**George W. Bush**

*"The only way to defeat the terrorists is to defeat their dark vision of hatred and fear by offering the hopeful alternative of political freedom."*

In the following viewpoint George W. Bush argues that bringing democracy to Middle Eastern nations can reduce conflict and promote peace. A lack of democracy in the region has led to terrorism, oppression, and war, says Bush. But democracy offers Middle Easterners the hope of freedom, political choice, and peace, he claims. Furthermore, Bush believes that America will benefit from bringing democracy to the Middle East because it will reduce anti-American sentiment and terrorism. Bush concludes that supporting democratic change in the Middle East will help the citizens of that region and the world.

George W. Bush is the forty-third president of the United States.

**AS YOU READ, CONSIDER THE FOLLOWING QUESTIONS:**

1. How many democratic nations are there in the world today, as reported by Bush?

George W. Bush, "State of the Union Address," The White House, January 31, 2006. Courtesy of The White House.

2. What democratic initiatives recently occurred in Egypt and among the Palestinians, according to Bush?
3. How might democracy help Iran, according to Bush?

A broad, our nation is committed to an historic, long-term goal—we seek the end of tyranny in our world. Some dismiss that goal as misguided idealism. In reality, the future security of America depends on it. On September the 11th, 2001, we found that problems originating in a failed and oppressive state 7,000 miles away could bring murder and destruction to our country. Dictatorships shelter terrorists, and feed resentment and radicalism, and seek weapons of mass destruction. Democracies replace resentment with hope, respect the rights of their citizens and their neighbors, and join the fight against terror. Every step toward freedom in the world makes our country safer—so we will act boldly in freedom's cause.

## Democracy Is Spreading to the Middle East

Far from being a hopeless dream, the advance of freedom is the great story of our time. In 1945, there were about two dozen lonely democracies in the world. Today, there are 122. And we're writing a new chapter in the story of self-government—with women lining up to vote in Afghanistan, and millions of Iraqis marking their liberty with purple ink, and men and women from Lebanon to Egypt debating the rights of individuals and the necessity of freedom. At the start of 2006, more than half the people of our world live in democratic nations. And we do not forget the other half—in places like Syria and Burma, Zimbabwe, North Korea, and Iran—because the demands of justice, and the peace of this world, require their freedom, as well.

No one can deny the success of freedom, but some men rage and fight against it. And one of the main sources of reaction and opposition is radical Islam—the perversion by a few of a noble faith into an ideology of terror and death. Terrorists like bin Laden are serious about mass murder—and all of us must take their declared intentions seriously. They seek to impose a heartless system of totalitarian control throughout the Middle East, and arm themselves with weapons of mass murder.

*President Bush believes that introducing democracy in the Middle East will bring freedom and choice, ultimately reducing terrorism around the world.*

Their aim is to seize power in Iraq, and use it as a safe haven to launch attacks against America and the world. Lacking the military strength to challenge us directly, the terrorists have chosen the weapon of fear. When they murder children at a school in Beslan [Russia], or blow up commuters in London, or behead a bound captive, the terrorists hope these horrors will break our will, allowing the violent to inherit the Earth. But they have miscalculated: We love our freedom, and we will fight to keep it.

## Democracy Abroad to Keep the Home Front Safe

In a time of testing, we cannot find security by abandoning our commitments and retreating within our borders. If we were to leave these vicious attackers alone, they would not leave us alone. They would simply move the battlefield to our own shores. There is no peace in retreat. And there is no honor in retreat. By allowing radical Islam to work its will—by leaving an assaulted world to fend for itself—we would signal to all that we no longer believe in our own ideals, or even in our own courage. But our enemies and our friends can be certain: The United States will not retreat from the world, and we will never surrender to evil.

America rejects the false comfort of isolationism. We are the nation that saved liberty in Europe, and liberated death camps, and helped raise up democracies, and faced down an evil empire. Once again, we accept the call of history to deliver the oppressed and move this world toward peace. We remain on the offensive against terror networks. We have killed or captured many of their leaders—and for the others, their day will come.

## Democratic Progress in Iraq

We remain on the offensive in Afghanistan, where a fine President and a National Assembly are fighting terror while building the institutions of a new democracy. We're on the offensive in Iraq, with a clear plan for victory. First, we're helping Iraqis build an inclusive government, so that old resentments will be eased and the insurgency will be marginalized.

Second, we're continuing reconstruction efforts, and helping the Iraqi government to fight corruption and build a modern economy, so all Iraqis can experience the benefits of freedom. And, third, we're striking terrorist targets while we train Iraqi forces that are increasingly capable of defeating the enemy. Iraqis are showing their courage every day, and we are proud to be their allies in the cause of freedom.

Our work in Iraq is difficult because our enemy is brutal. But that brutality has not stopped the dramatic progress of a new democracy. In less than three years, the nation has gone from dictatorship to liberation, to sovereignty, to a constitution, to national elections. At the same time, our coalition has been relentless in shutting off terrorist infiltration, clearing out insurgent strongholds, and turning

**FAST FACT**

According to the World Values Survey, 98.5 percent of Egyptians and 94.7 percent of Jordanians said they thought having a democratic government is very good or fairly good.

over territory to Iraqi security forces. I am confident in our plan for victory; I am confident in the will of the Iraqi people; I am confident in the skill and spirit of our military. Fellow citizens, we are in this fight to win, and we are winning.

The road of victory is the road that will take our troops home. As we make progress on the ground, and Iraqi forces increasingly take the lead, we should be able to further decrease our troop levels—but those decisions will be made by our military commanders, not by politicians in Washington, D.C. . . .

## Democracy Is the Key to Peace

Our offensive against terror involves more than military action. Ultimately, the only way to defeat the terrorists is to defeat their dark vision of hatred and fear by offering the hopeful alternative of political freedom and peaceful change. So the United States of America supports democratic reform across the broader Middle East. Elections are vital, but they are only the beginning. Raising up a democracy requires the rule of law, and protection of minorities, and strong, accountable institutions that last longer than a single vote.

The great people of Egypt have voted in a multi-party presidential election—and now their government should open paths of peaceful opposition that will reduce the appeal of radicalism. The Palestinian people have voted in elections. And now the leaders of Hamas must recognize Israel, disarm, reject terrorism, and work for lasting peace. Saudi Arabia has taken the first steps of reform—now it can offer its people a better future by pressing forward with those efforts. Democracies in the Middle East will not look like our own, because they will reflect the traditions of their own citizens. Yet liberty is the future of every nation in the Middle East, because liberty is the right and hope of all humanity.

## Building Democracy to Fight Terror

The same is true of Iran, a nation now held hostage by a small clerical elite that is isolating and repressing its people. The regime in that country sponsors terrorists in the Palestinian territories and in Lebanon—and that must come to an end. The Iranian government is defying the world with its nuclear ambitions, and the nations of the

# Arabs and Democracy

A World Values Survey taken of Egyptians and Jordanians revealed the following opinions of democracy:

## Having a democratic government is:

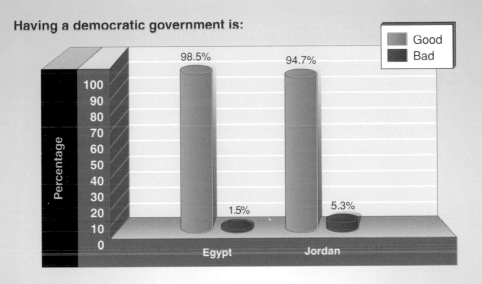

## Democracy is better than any other form of government:

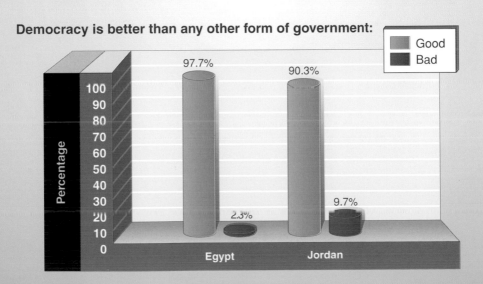

Source: ABC News / *Washington Post*, January 2003.

world must not permit the Iranian regime to gain nuclear weapons. America will continue to rally the world to confront these threats.

Tonight, let me speak directly to the citizens of Iran: America respects you, and we respect your country. We respect your right to choose your own future and win your own freedom. And our nation hopes one day to be the closest of friends with a free and democratic Iran.

## EVALUATING THE AUTHORS' ARGUMENTS:

In this viewpoint Bush argues that democracy will bring peace to the Middle East. But in the following viewpoint author Amir Taheri explains why he believes it will be impossible to implement democracy in Muslim nations. After reading both viewpoints, which author do you believe is correct about the role that democracy can play in bringing peace to the Middle East? Explain your position using examples from the text.

**Viewpoint**

**2**

# Democracy Cannot Bring Peace to the Middle East

**"The bottom line is that no Islamic government can be democratic in the sense of allowing the common people equal shares in legislation."**

### Amir Taheri

In the following viewpoint author Amir Taheri argues that democracy will not foster peace in the Middle East because democracy is incompatible with Islam, the majority religion in the region. Taheri lists several reasons why Islam and democracy cannot be mixed. For one, he explains, Islam does not advocate equality among all people, which is a fundamental tenet of democracy. Furthermore, democracy accords power to people, while Islam accords all power only to God. Islam also does not allow people the freedom to do whatever they want, and personal freedom is an important part of democracy. For all of these reasons, Taheri concludes that it will be impossible to implement democracy in Muslim nations, and thus it is not an effective tool for creating peace in the Middle East.

Taheri is an Iranian-born journalist. His writings focus on Middle East affairs and topics related to Islamic terrorism.

Amir Taheri, "Islam and Democracy: The Impossible Union," *The Sunday Times*, May 23, 2004. Reproduced by permission.

**AS YOU READ, CONSIDER THE FOLLOWING QUESTIONS:**
1. What is the closest word to "politics" in Muslim languages? What does it mean?
2. Why does the author say that Muslims should take as a compliment the idea that Islam is not compatible with democracy?
3. According to the author, how many of the fifty-seven nations in the Organization of the Islamic Conference are democracies?

I n recent weeks there has been much soul-searching, in the Islamic world and among the wider Muslim diaspora about whether Islam is compatible with democracy. . . . As an Iranian now living in a liberal democracy, I would like to explain why Islam and democracy are essentially incompatible.

## No Language Basis for Democracy

To understand a civilisation it is important to comprehend the language that shapes it. There was no word in any of the Muslim languages for democracy until the 1890s. Even then the Greek word entered Muslim vocabulary with little change: democrasi in Persian, dimokraytiyah in Arabic, demokratio in Turkish.

Democracy is based on one fundamental principle: equality. . . . We find no equivalent in any of the Muslim languages. The words we have such as barabari in Persian and sawiyah in Arabic mean juxtaposition or separation.

Nor do we have a word for politics. The word siassah, now used as a synonym for politics, initially meant whipping stray camels into line. (Sa'es al-kheil is a person who brings back lost camels to the caravan.) The closest translation may be: regimentation.

Nor is there mention of such words as government and the state in the Koran. Early Muslims translated numerous ancient Greek texts, but never those related to political matters.

## Equality Is Not a Feature of Islam

The idea of equality is unacceptable to Islam. For the non-believer cannot be the equal of the believer. Even among the believers only those who subscribe to the three Abrahamic religions: Judaism,

# Democracy in the Middle East

TURKEY

SYRIA

LEBANON —
ISRAEL —

IRAQ

IRAN

Israel is the only free country in the Middle East, according to the 2006 Freedom House survey Freedom in the World.

— JORDAN

KUWAIT
BAHRAIN —
QATAR —

EGYPT

SAUDI
ARABIA

U.A.E

— OMAN

Red Sea

SUDAN

YEMEN

Free country, in which citizens enjoy a high degree of political and civil freedom.

Partly free country, in which citizens endure some restrictions on political rights and civil liberties.

Not free country, in which the political process is tightly controlled and basic freedoms are denied.

Source: Freedom House, 2006.

**FAST FACT**

The number of democra-
cies in the world has grown
from just 40 in the 1970s
to more than 120 in the
twenty-first century.

Christianity and Islam, known as the "people of the book" (Ahl el-Kitab), are regarded as fully human. Here, too, there is a hierarchy, with Muslims at the top.

Non-Muslims can, and have often been, treated with decency, but never as equals. There is a hierarchy even for animals and plants. Seven animals and seven plants will assuredly go to heaven while seven others of each will end up in hell.

Democracy means the rule of the demos, the common people, or what is now known as popular or national sovereignty. In Islam, however, power belongs only to God: al-hukm l'illah. The man who exercises that power on Earth is known as Khalifat al-Allah, the regent of God. Even then the Khalifah, or Caliph, cannot act as legislator. The law has already been spelt out and fixed forever by God. . . .

The bottom line is that no Islamic government can be democratic in the sense of allowing the common people equal shares in legislation. Islam divides human activities into five categories, from the permitted to the sinful, leaving little room for human interpretation, let alone ethical innovations.

To say that Islam is incompatible with democracy should not be seen as a disparagement of Islam. On the contrary, many Muslims would see it as a compliment because they believe that their idea of rule by God is superior to that of rule by men, which is democracy. . . .

## Islamic Leaders Reject Democracy

Many Islamist thinkers regard democracy with horror.

The late Ayatollah Khomeini called democracy "a form of prostitution", because he who gets the most votes wins the power that belongs only to God.

Sayyid Qutb, the Egyptian who has emerged as the ideological mentor of Salafists (fundamentalists who want to return to the idyllic Islamic state of their forebears) spent a year in the United States in the 1950s. He found "a nation that has forgotten God and been forsaken by Him; an arrogant nation that wants to rule itself".

[In 2003] Yussuf al-Ayyeri, one of the leading theoreticians of today's Islamist movement, published a book in which he warned that the real danger to Islam did not come from American tanks and helicopter gunships in Iraq but from the idea of democracy and the government of the people.

Maudoodi, another of the Islamist theoreticians now fashionable, dreamt of a political system in which humans would act as automatons in accordance with rules set by God. He said that God has arranged man's biological functions in such a way that their operation is beyond human control. For our non-biological functions, notably our politics, God has also set rules that we have to discover and apply once and for all so that our societies can be on autopilot, so to speak.

## "The Curse of Democracy"
The late Saudi theologian, Sheikh Muhammad bin Ibrahim al-Jubair, a man I respected though seldom agreed with, believed that the root cause of contemporary ills was the spread of democracy.

"Only one ambition is worthy of Islam," he liked to say, "to save the world from the curse of democracy: to teach men that they cannot rule themselves on the basis of man-made laws. Mankind has strayed from the path of God, we must return to that path or face certain annihilation."

Those who claim that Islam is compatible with democracy should know that they are not flattering Muslims.

## Democracy Is Not the Answer
In the past 14 centuries Muslims have, on occasions, succeeded in creating successful societies without democracy. And there is no guarantee that democracy never produces disastrous results (after all, Hitler was democratically elected).

The fact that almost all Muslim states today can be rated as failures or, at least, underachievers, is not because they are Islamic but because they are ruled by corrupt and despotic elites that, even when they proclaim an Islamist ideology, are, in fact, secular dictators.

Socrates ridiculed the myth of democracy by pointing out that men always call on experts to deal with specific tasks, but when it comes to the more important matters concerning the community, they allow every Tom, Dick and Harry an equal say.

In response his contemporary, Protagoras, one of the original defenders of democracy, argued: "People in the cities, especially in Athens, listen only to experts in matters of expertise, but when they meet for consultation on the political art, ie of the general question of government, everybody participates."

*The Congress of Democrats from the Islamic World disagrees with those who believe that democracy is incompatible with Islam.*

## Islam Is Not Compatible with Democracy

Traditional Islamic political thought is closer to Socrates than to Protagoras. The common folk, al-awwam, are regarded as "animals". The interpretation of the divine law is reserved only for the experts. Political power, like many other domains, including philosophy, is reserved for the "khawas" who, in some Sufi traditions, are even exempt from the rituals of the faith.

The "common folk", however, must do as they are told either by the text and tradition or by fatwas (edicts) issued by the experts. Khomeini used the word "mustazafeen" (the feeble ones) to describe the general population.

Islam is about certainty (iqan) while democracy is about doubt. Islam cannot allow people to do as they please, even in the privacy of their bedrooms, because God is always present, all-hearing and all-seeing.

There is consultation in Islam: wa shawerhum fil amr (and consult them in matters). But, here, consultation is about specifics only, never about the overall design of society.

In democracy there is a constitution that can be amended or changed. The Koran, however, is the immutable word of God, beyond amendment or change. . . .

## Do Not Force Democracy on the Middle East

Depriving Islam of critical scrutiny is bad for Islam and Muslims, and ultimately dangerous for the whole world. There are 57 nations in the Organisation of the Islamic Conference (OIC). Not one is yet a democracy.

We should not allow the everything-is-equal-to-everything-else fashion of postmodernist multiculturalism and political correctness to prevent us from acknowledging differences and even incompatibilities in the name of a soggy consensus. If we are all the same, how can we have a dialogue of civilisations?

Muslims should not be duped into believing that they can have their cake and eat it. Muslims can build successful societies provided they treat Islam as a matter of personal, private belief and not as a political ideology that seeks to monopolise the public space shared by the whole of humanity and dictate every aspect of individual and community life. Islam is incompatible with democracy.

## EVALUATING THE AUTHOR'S ARGUMENTS:

In the viewpoint you just read, the author suggests Muslims should treat their religion as a personal, private matter and not as a political ideology. What do you think? Can religion work as a political ideology or be used as a basis for government, or should it be kept as a private and personal matter? Explain your position.

**Viewpoint 3**

# Creating a Palestinian State Will Bring Peace to the Middle East

## Michael Lerner

*"Who in their right mind would want this struggle between Israel and its Arab and Muslim neighbors to continue for decades to come?"*

In the following viewpoint author Michael Lerner suggests that peace cannot come to the Middle East until a Palestinian state is created. Denying the Palestinians their own state and refusing to pay reparations for past wrongs is a continual source of anger, terrorism, and war in the region, says Lerner. At the same time, Lerner states that such a Palestinian state must recognize the right of Israel to exist and refrain from promoting terrorism. Creating a Palestinian state would send a powerful message that peace and justice prevail over terrorism and war, he argues. Lerner concludes that such a message has the power to change the political atmosphere of the entire world.

Michael Lerner is a rabbi, political activist, and the editor of *Tikkun*, a left-wing Jewish magazine based in San Francisco, from which this viewpoint was taken.

Michael Lerner, "When Will They Ever Learn?: How to Overcome the Middle East Mess," *Tikkun*, p. 8. Copyright 2006 *Tikkun* Magazine. Reproduced by permission of *Tikkun*: A Bimonthly Jewish Critique of Politics, Culture & Society.

**AS YOU READ, CONSIDER THE FOLLOWING QUESTIONS:**
1. What borders does Lerner propose for a Palestinian state?
2. What do extremists have to gain by preventing peace, in the author's opinion?
3. In what way does Lerner think creating a Palestinian state could improve the image of the United States?

A part from those oil companies who find themselves with windfall profits each time the price of petroleum rises, and who have thus been enriched whenever Middle East conflict tells the global capitalist market that there is a risk of oil shortages and thus encourages them to raise prices, and apart from Christian fundamentalist fanatics who actually celebrated when the war between Israel and Hezbollah broke out in July, 2006, imagining that this was a sign that the ultimate war of Gog and Magog was closer and hence the Apocalypse and Second Coming of Jesus was around the corner, who in their right mind would want this struggle between Israel and its Arab and Muslim neighbors to continue for decades to come?

## Extremists Do Not Want Peace

Only extremist nuts, who should not be allowed to prevail.

And yet, that is precisely what will happen unless the international community broadens its current concern with enforcing a cease-fire, and working out new border arrangements between Israel and Hezbollah that would prevent either side from encroaching on the other. What is needed is for the world to impose on Israel and the Arab states a permanent, sustainable, and just settlement so that the peoples of that troubled region can stop fighting and start cooperating to build a thriving economy and cooperative and safe neighborhoods for all of its peoples.

Why impose? Because there are extremists on all sides of this struggle who would prefer to keep it going for the next hundred years rather than give up their maximalist fantasies of decisively defeating the other sides. Extremists in Israel, Syria, Hezbollah, Hamas, and Iran each have the capacity to commit provocative acts that would give extremists on the other sides apparent justification to escalate into new wars and violence—thereby thwarting the wishes of the majorities in Israel, Palestine, Lebanon, and Syria who would prefer peace to endless war.

## The Terms of Palestinian Statehood

The terms are clear:

- Creation of a Palestinian state encompassing all of the West Bank and Gaza, with minor border alterations to allow Israel to incorporate some of the settlements directly adjacent to its borders, and the Jewish and Armenian quarters of the Old City in Jerusalem, in exchange for an equal amount of land to be given to Palestine from what is now Israel. Simultaneously, there must be unequivocal recognition of the right of Israel to exist as a Jewish state (in the same way that there are many Muslim states in the region) as long as there is documentable anti-Semitism facing communities of Jews around the world, and as long as Israel, apart from offering special immigration rights to Jews fleeing from elsewhere because of reasonable fears of persecution, offers fully equal rights to its minority populations. Palestine will offer similar special immigration privileges to Palestinians from around the world, and similar rights to its minorities (including any Jewish settlers who choose to remain in their settlements as law-abiding citizens of Palestine).
- An international consortium to fund reparations for Palestinian refugees who lost property or livelihood from 1947–2006, and for Jewish refugees from Arab lands, who lost property or livelihood from 1948–2006.
- An international force to work in close cooperation with Israel and Palestine to provide security from terrorists, and to protect both countries from each other and from any other outside forces that might seek to attack or control either country.
- International supervision of the regional media, education system, textbooks, and religious institutions to ensure that there is a total ban on teaching or encouraging hatred or denigration of the other.
- A Truth and Reconciliation process similar to that which took place in South Africa. And referral to an international war crimes

tribunal for any who do not publicly confess their acts of violence and human rights abuses.

## Practicing the Language of Peace

So why doesn't this happen? Because the political realists who shape public discourse in most countries focus our attention on the tiny little steps they imagine can be achieved in the short run, rather than supporting the dramatic changes that are needed to save the Middle East from endless war, or, for that matter, the changes that are needed to save our planet from nuclear war and environmental catastrophe.

*Israeli peace activists demonstrate against violence by Jewish settlers toward Palestinians in Hebron.*

What is needed is a new discourse that teaches Jews, Arabs, Muslims, Americans, Europeans, Chinese, Japanese, Russians, and everyone else on the planet that we need a New Bottom Line and a new way of thinking about politics, starting with the following three guidelines: 1. Our well being as Americans depends on the well-being of everyone else on the planet. Policies that seek to privilege one group without taking into account the needs of others are reckless and irresponsible. We are one family of humanity; we are all in this together. And so our economic, social, political, environmental, education and religious policies and practices must reflect this fundamental truth of the oneness and interconnectedness of all human beings on the planet with each other and with the planet on which we live. 2. The path to peace must in fact be peaceful. Non-violence is not just the goal, but also the means. 3. Every human being is equally precious. There can never be "moral equivalence" between any unnecessary death and any other—because every human being on the planet is infinitely precious.

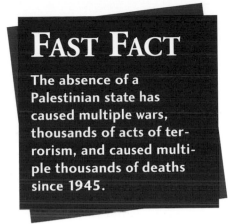

## A Chance to Change the World

So what could the U.S. and Israel do to change the whole dynamics of politics in the world? First, acknowledge that we have pursued policies that have, either intentionally or unintentionally, hurt many people and done damage to the world, publicly repent and ask forgiveness for those whom we have hurt (including the families of those who have been killed by the war in Iraq and the war in Palestine). Second, lead the G8 countries in a massive "Global Marshall Plan" in which we dedicate 5 percent of our Gross Domestic Product each year for the next twenty to eliminating global poverty, hunger, homelessness, inadquate education and inadequate health care, delivered in ways that assure that the monies reach the people and cannot be skimmed off by governmental or economic elites, and implemented

# What Would a Palestinian State Look Like?

Beirut

Damascus

**LEBANON**

Litani River

**GOLAN HEIGHTS**
(Syrian territory occupied
by Israel in 1967)

Jordan River

Lake
Tiberias

Yarmuk River

**SYRIA**

**JORDAN**

Tel Aviv

**WEST
BANK**

Amman

Jericho

Jerusalem

Mediterranean
Sea

Gaza

**GAZA
STRIP**

Dead
Sea

There are several proposals
for what land might comprise
a Palestinian state, but most
proposals include the territories
known as the Gaza Strip and
the West Bank. Palestinians
also insist that Jerusalem be
included in their state, but Israel
has thus far held tightly to its
claim on the Holy City.

**ISRAEL**

**EGYPT**

----  Armistice Demarcation Line, 1949

Palestinian territory occupied by
Israel (June 1967)

Source: William N. Dale, "Middle East Water Problems," *American Diplomacy*, 2001.
www.unc.edu/depts/diplomat/archives_roll/2001_07-09/dale_water/dale_water.html.

in ways that are culturally and ecologically sensitive. Third, have our elected leaders spend the next two years visiting the households of people in Iraq, Haiti, Palestine, Lebanon and Israel whose lives have been lost because of our policies, to personally ask for forgiveness. Fourth, reject the notion that everyone is out to hurt us, and instead talk to the world of a Spirit of Generosity that will from now on be the guiding principle in our foreign policy.

## A Palestinian State Will Improve America's Image

If Israel implements the peace plan and the U.S. starts the Global Marshall Plan, within five years there will be a decisive shift in the way that the majority of people of the world respond to us. Within ten years, that shift will be significant enough that terrorists will have a much tougher time recruiting volunteers to destroy themselves. In fact, this approach is actually far more likely to work than any policies currently being proposed by anyone in the self-described "realistic" versions of politics that dominate most of the currents of discourse on Left, Right and center in America and Israel. Our job is to spread this vision, reject the idolatry of "cynical realism," and reaffirm that the world can be built on love and generosity—a message even more realistic today and even more needed. When will the powerful ever learn that the ancient wisdom of the prophets and spiritual teachers of the past 4,000 years are more pressingly needed today? It's pointless to wait for some magical candidate or orator—this is OUR mission, and you and I, dear reader, have to take it seriously.

### EVALUATING THE AUTHOR'S ARGUMENTS:

The author of this viewpoint, Michael Lerner, is a Jewish rabbi, and his article was published in the Jewish journal *Tikkun*. Does it surprise you that a Jew would argue in support of the creation of a Palestinian state? Why or why not? Explain your reasoning.

# Creating a Palestinian State Will Cause Further Conflict

*"The international community must unite behind a diplomatic siege and an active boycott of the [Palestinian Authority]."*

**Moshe Yaalon**

In the following viewpoint author Moshe Yaalon argues that a Palestinian state led by the wrong government could cause further conflict in the Middle East. He discusses the 2006 Palestinian elections in which representatives from the terrorist group Hamas won control of the Palestinian Authority, the governing organization in the Palestinian Territories. The Hamas win spells disaster for peace initiatives in the region, according to Yaalon. At the helm of Palestinian leadership, Hamas will likely increase Palestinian ties with terrorist organizations, increase attacks on Israel, and undermine peace efforts throughout the Middle East. Yaalon urges the international community to reject any Palestinian state that would be led by terrorist groups such as Hamas.

Moshe Yaalon is a retired lieutenant general who served in the Israeli army.

Moshe Yaalon, PolicyWatch No. 1080: Special Forum Report, Washington, DC: Washington Institute for Near East Policy, 2006. Reproduced by permission.

**AS YOU READ, CONSIDER THE FOLLOWING QUESTIONS:**
  1. According to Yaalon, which terrorist groups will be aided by a Hamas-led Palestinian state?
  2. How does a Hamas-led Palestine threaten Arab states such as Egypt and Jordan, in Yaalon's opinion?
  3. What does Yaalon say the Palestinian people knew about Hamas when they elected it?

Hamas's recent victory in the Palestinian parliamentary elections challenges all those actors currently invested in promoting change in the Middle East. These include Israel, Western nations, Arab democrats, and Palestinian moderates. Adding to this challenge is the perception of radical Islamists—Sunni and Shiite alike—that Hamas's victory is a defeat for U.S. policy in the region, a blow to democratization, and a victory for Islamist fundamentalism.

Addressing the implications of Hamas's victory demands a clear understanding of these challenges. Regarding Israel and the United States's approach toward the Palestinian Authority (PA), Hamas leader Khalid Mishal's recent speech at a Damascus mosque should be clarifying. Mishal said: "The nation of Islam will sit at the throne of the world, and the West will be full of remorse." This language—and particularly Mishal's references to "the nation of Islam" and "the West"—mirrors that of Osama bin Laden and Iranian president Mahmoud Ahmadinezhad. It is therefore not sufficient to say that Hamas's victory is simply a Palestinian popular response to Fatah corruption; it must be viewed, more accurately, as a victory for radical Islamism, as perceived by radical Islamists globally.

## A Hamas-Led Palestinian State Will Promote Terrorism

There are three primary security implications of Hamas's electoral victory. First and foremost is the morale encouragement it provides to terrorists and rogue regimes—including al-Qaeda, global Jihad organizations, Syria, and Iran. The election will, quite dangerously, inspire Muslim Brotherhood affiliates in pro-Western regimes, including Egypt and Jordan. It will further energize the imaginations of Muslims everywhere, unifying Muslims under the banner of radical Islam, rather than drawing them to the flag of democratization being waved by the United States and the West.

Second, Hamas's victory will improve cooperation among the Hamas-led PA, Hamas terror apparatuses, Palestinian terrorist organizations, Iran, and al-Qaeda. Recent meetings between Mishal and Ahmadinezhad in Damascus should be viewed as early warnings of this dangerous alliance, which will grow with or without Western financial backing of the Hamas-led government. This partnership will overlook differences between Sunni Hamas and Shiite Iran, reflecting the common interests of anti-Western radicalism, and Palestinian terrorist organizations will benefit from newfound Iranian funding, terrorist mentorship, weapons systems, and ammunition. This situation has already begun to unfold: Hizballah has moved operational headquarters from Beirut to Gaza, while operating terror cells in the West Bank and Gaza; its ability to operate will only increase once Hamas officially takes power.

'A REPRESENTATIVE FROM THE NEW PALESTINIAN GOVERNMENT TO SEE YOU, MR. PRESIDENT'

Third, al-Qaeda elements, which Hamas will permit to operate as proxies, will increasingly penetrate the PA. Currently, al-Qaeda elements are exploiting an unstable situation by recruiting frustrated Fatah activists and former Hamas terrorists opposing the *tahdiya* (period of calm). . . .

## The Threat to Arab Nations

*Egypt.* As a consequence of Hamas's victory, Egypt must worry about a potential boost for the Egyptian Muslim Brotherhood. Egypt will further face increased Iranian and al-Qaeda involvement and influence in the PA, particularly in Gaza. This may force the Egyptian regime to demonstrate more determination in thwarting weapons smugglers and terrorists in Sinai. However, it will not be surprising if Egypt reaches an understanding with Hamas to the benefit of both parties; this will undermine Israeli security objectives.

*Jordan.* Although less threatened than Egypt, Jordan will likewise face the danger of increased Iranian involvement in the PA, and the West Bank may become a platform for undermining the Hashemite regime.

## Encouraging Partners in Terrorism

*Syria.* Syrian president Bashar al-Asad is satisfied by Hamas's victory, viewing it as a defeat both for Israel and U.S. policy. Asad believes that Hamas's victory will provide him leverage for advancing Syrian interests and reducing international pressure. Encouraged by Hamas's success, Syria will continue supporting Hizballah and Palestinian terrorist organizations to serve Syrian interests with fewer restraints.

*Iran.* Clearly, Hamas's victory is a boost for the Iranian regime. Iran will likely exploit Hamas's victory by penetrating the PA; its increased influence will give it more options

**FAST FACT**

According to the Council on Foreign Relations, Hamas, the group elected by Palestinians in 2006, is believed to have killed more than five hundred Israelis in more than 350 separate terrorist attacks since 1993.

*Palestinians celebrated when Hamas members won control of the Palestian Authority. Others around the world expressed concern for peace efforts.*

against Israel. The Palestinian arena might be a more convenient Iranian platform than Lebanon, and Iran will use it to encourage terror activities against moderate regimes in Egypt, Jordan, and the PA. This new option might be used as leverage against the West in pursuing its nuclear ambitions.

## Undermine the Palestinian Government

Hamas's victory in the Palestinian parliamentary elections will likely spawn a counter "earthquake" to the U.S.-led push for democratization, which will not be confined to the Palestinian internal arena or the Israeli-Palestinian conflict. It must be dealt with as such. In this vein, the United States and the international community should realize that the Israeli-Palestinian track has completely lost its way; they should return to the sentiments expressed by President George W. Bush in his June 24, 2002, address to guide them toward a policy of isolating the PA so long as it is compromised by terror. The Roadmap was a detour from this policy.

The only way to address the problems created by a Hamas-led PA is to undermine its authority as soon as possible. Indeed, time is running out: Iran, al-Qaeda, and other Islamist elements will quickly exploit the situation, and they will have greater opportunity to do so given Israel's withdrawal from Gaza. A clear Israeli strategy, supported by the international community, is necessary in order to compel a positive change in the PA, either toward moderation (if that is possible) or collapse (if moderation does not occur). We should not fear collapse; the experience of Israel's security operations in recent years shows that Palestinian society will not collapse—as the word is commonly interpreted—even under extreme conditions. Municipalities, for example, continued to operate and provide services even at the height of Israel military actions against the PA.

## The World to Palestine: "Terrorism Does Not Pay"

The preconditions for legitimating Hamas have been established. Until these conditions are met, the international community must unite behind a diplomatic siege and an active boycott of the PA. Israel should freeze its economic agreements with the PA on border procedures and further intensify its military counterterrorism activities, especially in Gaza. The only restraint should be avoiding a humanitarian crisis, which can be done through working with municipalities and non-governmental institutions. The mistake that allowed Hamas to participate in the elections without preconditions has brought us to this point. Without working to correct it, the situation will not improve.

It must be remembered that the Palestinian people elected Hamas with full awareness of its terrorist nature. It is therefore highly important that the international community send a clear message that terrorism does not pay. Such a statement will serve to undermine terrorists and their supporters worldwide. At the same time, it will provide a much-needed boost to those prodemocracy moderates who reject terrorism.

# Chapter 3

# What Role Should the United States Play in the Middle East?

*Some antiwar protesters feel that the U.S. should not be engaged in the Middle East conflict.*

**Viewpoint**

**1**

# The United States Should Negotiate with Terrorists

**Glen Moyer**

> *"Love and forgiveness are the ultimate weapons of war; . . . they are the only way to stop the endless cycle of vengeance and violence."*

In the following viewpoint Glen Moyer urges President George W. Bush to change the U.S. policy of not negotiating with terrorists. Moyer argues that not negotiating with terrorists will not result in peace and can hurt the image of America in the Muslim world. Although terrorists are murderers, Moyer believes that attempting to engage them in dialogue may resolve some of the issues that spur them to commit terrorism. Moyer also suggests that terrorists can be reformed and points out that the United States used to be a nation that enslaved its people and murdered natives in order to illegally take land. If the United States can change, he reasons, so can terrorists. He urges Bush to negotiate with terrorists in an attempt to end the cycle of violence and vengeance that fuels conflict in the Middle East.

Moyer is pastor of High Point Adventures. He mailed this letter to Bush on February 28, 2006.

Glen Moyer, "Maybe It's Time to Negotiate with the Enemy," *The Missoulian* (Montana), March 6, 2006. Copyright 2006 Missoulian, a division of Lee Enterprises. Reproduced by permission.

**AS YOU READ, CONSIDER THE FOLLOWING QUESTIONS:**
1. In the author's opinion, has the war on terror strengthened or weakened al Qaida?
2. How should the government have handled Osama bin Laden's November 2005 invitation to negotiate a truce, in Moyer's opinion?
3. What does the phrase "the high road" mean in the context of the viewpoint?

D ear President Bush,
I'd like to ask you to reconsider our diplomatic position with the extremist Islamic group al-Qaida.

First, I'm not a flaming liberal. Second, I'm not a flaming conservative. Third, I'm not a flaming idiot—at least I don't think so. I'm just a dude who has come to the conclusion that we can go in a better direction.

## Not Negotiating Has Not Worked

Our current policy says: "We do not negotiate with terrorists." I understand this position in situations such as when the Popular Front for the Liberation of Palestine hijacked several planes and passengers in 1970, or the Iranian Hostage Crisis of 1979–1981, or even in recent situations such as when Islamic extremists in Iraq kidnapped American construction worker Nicholas Berg in 2004 and beheaded him. Giving in to unreasonable demands of radical groups in situations like these would only create more copycat acts of violence.

However, our current posture with al-Qaida is not the same as one of those isolated, stand-off, lose-lose situations. We are, as you've stated in so many words, engaged in a long, difficult battle with Islamic extremists like al-Qaida on a global basis.

## FAST FACT

In a *FOX News/Opinion Dynamics* poll taken in April 2006, 30 percent of Americans believed the United States should try to negotiate with countries that back terrorism.

That said, neither is our posture with al-Qaida equivalent to our long global battles with Japan, Italy and Germany during World War II. Those were overt land battles where our enemies blatantly invaded nations with the goal of destroying the government and assuming control of the land and people.

Though I don't doubt for one second that radical factions such as al-Qaida would invade and conquer "infidel" nations if they only had the resources, the fact is they don't and can't. As a result they are waging the only war they can, a war of ideology, perpetuated by frequent and random acts of violence.

As a result, far from disappearing from the radar, al-Qaida is every bit the enemy they were before we declared war against them and more. They are achieving advances because our current diplomatic position plays perfectly into their strategy. As long as we continue as we are, so will al-Qaida.

Thus, my suggestion that we adopt a different diplomatic approach.

## We Should Accept Invitations to Talk

As you recall, in a November 2005 tape which the CIA confirmed was the voice of [9/11 mastermind] Osama bin Laden, he said, "We do not mind offering you a truce that is fair and long-term . . . so we can build Iraq and Afghanistan . . . there is no shame in this solution because it prevents wasting of billions of dollars."

Immediately, your press secretary said, I assume on your behalf, "We do not negotiate with terrorists. We put them out of business." Vice President [Dick] Cheney said to Fox News, "I don't think anybody would believe him. . . . It sounds to me like it's some kind of a ploy. . . . "

In a war of words we let bin Laden have the last word, again. We also ensured that this current spiral of violence continues. And finally, we made it look to the Muslim world like it's our entire fault.

## Terrorists Can Change

Why not come to the table with al-Qaida? Could anything be more empowering to our cause than to engage them with their own weapons—words? And what if bin Laden does want peace? Such changes can happen to people. After all, we are the same nation that

*President Bush's policy of nonnegotiation with terrorists may make it harder to achieve peace in the Middle East.*

oversaw the genocide of our own Native peoples and sanctioned the slavery of blacks for two centuries. Who are we to say that people like Osama bin Laden and al-Qaida can't change?

Finally, as a man of faith, I'm sure you know that Jesus modeled humility and forgiveness. Jesus refused to embrace the logic of, "If someone hits you, hit back! If anyone takes your coat, burn down his house!" No, Jesus said turn the other cheek, never stop forgiving and love your enemies.

He then laid down his innocent life out of love for his enemies, us. Even as he was being executed, Jesus said, "Father, forgive them; they don't know what they're doing" (Luke 23:34). Jesus knew that love and forgiveness are the ultimate weapons of war; that they are the only way to stop the endless cycle of vengeance and violence.

Again, I'm not saying that there is never a time to take up the sword. However, in the battle of words and ideology with al-Qaida, someone has to take the high road. Why not us? Why not negotiate with terrorists? Indeed, why not forgive terrorists?

Just as you and I have been transformed from enemies to friends with God, perhaps by loving and forgiving, or at the very least, talking with al-Qaida we may one day become friends with them. Nothing is impossible with God.

**EVALUATING THE AUTHOR'S ARGUMENTS:**

In this viewpoint Moyer draws on religious teachings to argue that terrorists should be forgiven despite the acts of murder they have committed. He believes that forgiving terrorists could open dialogue that will lead to peaceful resolution of conflict instead of the continuation of war. What do you think? Should the United States turn the other cheek and forgive terrorists in order to open a dialogue with them? What are the pros and cons of this position? Explain your reasoning.

# The United States Should Not Negotiate with Terrorists

**Darrell Puls**

> *"One cannot negotiate with those who find great pleasure in slaughtering thousands of innocents at a time . . . and readily kill themselves as part of the process."*

In the following viewpoint author Darrell Puls argues that the United States should never negotiate with terrorists. Because suicide terrorists do not value their own lives, he explains, they have nothing to lose, and thus will never give up something in exchange for something else, which is the core feature of negotiations. By negotiating with terrorists, the United States will only weaken its position and teach terrorists that their tactics are effective for getting what they want. Puls concludes that negotiating with terrorists is not effective behavior for resolving conflicts in the Middle East.

Darrell Puls is a professional mediator, negotiator, and trainer who lives in Kennewick, Washington. He has twenty-six years' experience in the field of conflict resolution. He has also written for Mediate.com, a conflict resolution Web site from which this viewpoint was taken.

**AS YOU READ, CONSIDER THE FOLLOWING QUESTIONS:**
1. Describe three terrorist plots mentioned by the author.
2. What situation does the author call "suicide by cop"?
3. How did negotiating hurt America in the Vietnam War, according to Puls?

Washington Mediation Association President Cris Currie writes on the Mediate.com website that we should be willing to negotiate with all, including terrorists. Indeed, the premise seems to be that we will find reason at the end of the tunnel if we just acknowledge the basic legitimacy of certain governments, regardless of how repulsive their actions, and the fundamental need of all humans to be accepted, regardless of their motivation. . . .

I have been a professional negotiator for 26 years and a mediator for 12. I served in the Army during the Vietnam War and have also been a police officer and am an FBI-trained hostage negotiator. I bring a different perspective to this discourse, and I differ with Mr. Currie.

## Terrorists Are a Different Kind of Enemy

First, I believe it is an error to compare the Gulf War with the current situation in Afghanistan and elsewhere in the world. We were dealing with a conventional army that had military objectives that largely did not include annihilating large civilian populations in Kuwait. The Gulf War was a mostly conventional battle between armored divisions, infantry and air forces, even though there were elements of terror. The objectives of the Iraqi army, if not the political leadership, were to gain control of Kuwaiti oil fields and open access to the sea. While there were aberrations along the way, the process was mostly conventional land and air warfare.

Al Qaeda, and the Taliban where it found succor, are completely different and not analogous. The terrorists first tried to kill upwards of 50,000 people by toppling the World Trade Center through the massive use of explosives in the underground parking garage in 1991. A plot to crash an airliner into the Eiffel Tower was foiled. Al Qaeda is now implicated in the murder of hundreds of our sons and brothers through unprovoked bombing attacks on the Marines, our embassies, and the USS *Cole*. Mr. bin Laden has now taken credit for the slaughter of thousands of innocents on September 11, crowing that the results were better than expected. The tape is clear and unequivocal—he was the primary person responsible.

## You Can't Negotiate with Those Who Prefer Death

Mr. Currie states, "(O)ne person's 'terrorist' is another's 'freedom fighter'." That may be true. It is also irrelevant. A label is just that and means nothing by itself and it certainly does not offer the cloak of legitimacy. There is an old axiom that actions speak louder than words, and when there is dissonance between them we must judge by what is done, not what is said. That someone might call them "freedom fighters" does not confer legitimacy nor should we proffer that mantle by offering to settle this amicably. Mr. bin Laden and his cohorts by their actions have chosen their destiny: surrender or die.

*Some believe that negotiating with terrorists like Hamas suicide bombers will validate their tactics and lead to increased violence.*

Hostage negotiators must rely on one basic assumption—the perpetrator wants to live more than he wants to die. Even so, the negotiation is done with snipers and SWAT teams ready to move the second the situation goes sour. It is no different here. The entire concept of jihad runs counter to this basic negotiation assumption, for to die as a martyr in jihad is a glorious thing that gives instant entrance to heaven. One cannot negotiate with those who find great pleasure in slaughtering thousands of innocents at a time, who see this as a holy mission, who want to die in the execution of said mission and readily kill themselves as part of the process. . . .

## It Is Too Late for Bargaining

I quickly learned on the street as a police officer that my brain through talk was my most useful weapon. I also learned that when talk failed and violence escalated my job was to neutralize the perpetrator as a

© 2004 by Monte Wolverton and CagleCartoons.com. All rights reserved.

threat as quickly and efficiently as possible. Finally, I learned that one could not talk with someone who is physically attacking you, is intent on killing you, and just as intent on dying in the process. We called it "suicide by cop." The western definition of that action is insanity, not worldview.

Mr. Currie, on the other hand, . . . posits, "But shouldn't the enemy have to give something for

this kind of acceptance? No, bargaining over acceptance is like bargaining over apology: acceptance is only effective when freely given, not when it's withheld. It is coercive to use acceptance as a bargaining chip. . . . " It is not coercive to defend oneself against an elusive enemy bent on killing as many of us as possible. There comes a time and place when an enemy forfeits the right to equality at a bargaining table, or even the right to approach the bargaining table.

## Negotiating Hurt America in the Past

[Philosopher George] Santayana remarked that those who do not learn from history are condemned to repeat it. History shows us clearly that negotiations are not only futile, but also even foolish in certain instances. As an illustration, it took two years for United States and Vietnamese negotiators to reach agreement on the shape of the bargaining table for the peace talks in Paris. During that time, the North Vietnamese continued to consolidate their gains. We only reached true negotiations during the massive bombing raids over Hanoi and Haiphong.

Negotiations bogged down again after the raids ended. The Vietnamese knew of our need to be understood through talk and capitalized on it, resulting in the deaths of thousands more of our sons and brothers.

President Teddy Roosevelt put it succinctly when he cautioned the nation to speak softly and carry a big stick. Why? Sometimes it is appropriate to speak softly—and sometimes to use the big stick.

## EVALUATING THE AUTHORS' ARGUMENTS:

In this viewpoint the author argues that negotiating with terrorists is a fruitless and foolish enterprise. The author of the previous viewpoint disagrees, arguing that negotiating with terrorists can be effective and beneficial. After reading both viewpoints, what is your opinion on whether the United States should negotiate with terrorists? Use material from the text to support your answer.

# The United States Should Withdraw from Iraq

*"We don't want U.S. troops remaining in the region and poised to go back into Iraq. They don't belong there, period."*

## Gilbert Achcar and Stephen R. Shalom

In the following viewpoint authors Gilbert Achcar and Stephen R. Shalom call for the complete withdrawal of American troops from Iraq. They believe that the presence of American troops in Iraq violates that nation's sovereignty and is against the will of the Iraqi people. Furthermore, the authors argue that troops should not be stationed nearby to monitor the situation—they claim such an arrangement would make the United States seem imperialist and would foster anti-U.S. sentiment. The authors conclude the United States should withdraw its troops in a timely and organized fashion.

Gilbert Achcar is the author of *The Clash of Barbarisms* and *Eastern Cauldron*. Stephen R. Shalom is the author of *Imperial Alibis* and serves on the editorial board of the journal *New Politics*, from which this viewpoint was taken.

There is much of which to approve in the [November 2005] speech of Rep. John P. Murtha, Democrat of Pennsylvania, on Iraq. The hawkish Murtha had been critical of the Bush administration's handling of the war for some time, but until now his solution had been to call for more troops. On November 17, however, he recognized courageously that U.S. troops "cannot accomplish anything further in Iraq militarily. *It is time to bring them home.*"

## U.S. Troops Add to Instability in Iraq

Murtha pointed out, as the antiwar movement has been pointing out all along, that the U.S. troops in Iraq, rather than adding to stability, "have become a catalyst for violence." He referred to the acknowledgement made by General George W. Casey, commander of the "multinational force" in Iraq, during a hearing before the Armed Services Committee of the U.S. Senate in September, 2005, that the presence of "the coalition forces as an occupying force" is "one of the elements that fuels the insurgency." . . .

The antiwar movement cannot endorse U.S. military intervention in the Middle East, whether over or under the horizon. We don't want U.S. troops remaining in the region and poised to go back into Iraq. They don't belong there, period. Some—though not Murtha—suggest keeping U.S. bases within Iraq, close to the oil fields or in Kurdistan, in order to intervene

FAST FACT

A June 2006 Gallup poll found that 56 percent of Americans thought the Iraq war was not worth the cost, and 59 percent said some or all U.S. troops should be pulled out.

*It has been suggested that the presence of American troops in Iraq has led to an increase in violence in the region.*

more or less on the pattern of what U.S. forces are doing in Afghanistan. But this is a recipe for disaster, since the Iraqi view that the United States intends a permanent occupation is one of the main causes inciting the insurgency. Moreover, stationing U.S. forces in Kurdistan could only deepen the already dangerous ethnic animosities among Iraqis. In any event, if U.S. troops continue to be used in Iraq—whether deployed from bases inside the country or from outside—they will inevitably continue to cause civilian casualties, further provoking violence. Having a U.S. interventionary force stationed in Kuwait or in a similar location will continue to inflame the opposition of Iraqis who will know their sovereignty is still subject to U.S. control. As for the impact of keeping U.S. forces anywhere else in the larger region, it should be recalled that their presence was the decisive factor leading to 9-11 and fuels "global terrorism" in the same way that the U.S. military presence in Iraq "fuels the insurgency" there. . . .

The antiwar movement should and no doubt will relentlessly continue its fight for the immediate, total, and unconditional withdrawal of U.S. troops and their allies from Iraq and the whole region. Its central slogan "Troops Out Now" is more warranted each day and will keep gaining in urgency until victory over the warmongers is achieved. . . .

## We Must Insist on Total Withdrawal

It is possible that the U.S. will fall back on a strategy of trying to replace its troops with air power, hoping that the reduction in United States casualties will make the war more palatable to the American public. In late August [2005], the head of the air force told the *New York Times* that after any withdrawal of U.S. ground troops, "we will continue with a rotational presence of some type in that area more or less indefinitely," adding "We have interests in that part of the world. . . . " (Eric Schmitt, "U.S. General Says Iraqis Will Need Longtime Support from Air Force," Aug. 30) To support these interests Washington is upgrading 16 different bases in the Middle East and Southwest Asia (*New York Times*, Sept. 18, 2005). According to Seymour Hersh in the Dec. 5 *New Yorker*, plans are being drawn up precisely to replace U.S. ground troops in Iraq with warplanes. Hersh reports that some Pentagon officials are worried about what it would mean to have Iraqis calling in bombing targets to the U.S. Air Force, but no matter who calls in the coordinates, white phosphorus, cluster munitions, and 500-pound bombs are not going to address the problem of the insurgency; indeed, they are going to generate more recruits for both the insurgency and terrorism.

For the antiwar movement, it is critical to insist on the complete withdrawal of U.S. and coalition forces, from Iraq and from the region, because retaining any of them—whether counterinsurgency units ready to intervene or air power to level further Iraqi cities—will violate Iraqi sovereignty and continue to fuel insurgency and hatred. And the antiwar movement must insist as well on immediate withdrawal, because the Bush administration itself will soon be talking of future drawdowns—and indeed it already is. . . .

## It Is Possible to Withdraw in an Orderly Fashion

We are not calling for a "cut and run" withdrawal, abandoning Iraq to its fate (like in the "selfish" nationalist rhetoric of the isolationist Right). We are perfectly aware that, given what the United States has been doing in Iraq, tragically disrupting the situation in that country, if the U.S. troops were just to leave Iraq suddenly, say in 48 hours, without prior notice, that would definitely create a dangerous chaotic situation. But this is not what we are demanding. The demand for the immediate withdrawal of the troops is, first of all, a demand for an immediate political decision to withdraw the troops. Once the political decision is taken and proclaimed publicly, it becomes possible, in fact indispensable, to prepare the best conditions for its implementation in the shortest possible timeframe, while starting without delay to bring troops back home. To be sure, the modalities through which this should be completed in a way not to harm the Iraqi people must be worked out with their elected representatives.

If Washington were to make clear that it wants to complete the withdrawal of its troops within a timetable stretching over weeks, or very few months, this would provide a very powerful incentive for the Iraqis to reach an agreement among themselves on a way to run their

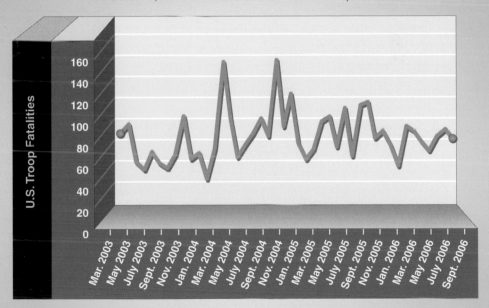

## U.S. Troop Fatalities

More than 2,500 soldiers have been killed in Iraq since 2003.

**Total from March 19, 2003 (start of major combat operations) through October 18, 2006:**
Fatalities (all kinds): **2,772**
Fatalities in hostile incidents: **2,217**
Fatalities in non-hostile incidents: **555**

Source: Michael E. O'Hanlon, "Iraq Index: Tracking Variables of Reconstruction & Security in Post-Saddam Iraq," Brookings Institution, October 19, 2006. www.brookings.edu/iraqindex.

country together peacefully and start to concentrate their efforts on the huge task of its reconstruction. The consensus reached at the November 2005 Cairo conference is an important step in that direction and proves that it is perfectly possible, and much easier indeed, to reach such agreements when U.S. representatives are not there constantly interfering and calling the shots.

## A Moral Obligation

Finally, those who accuse the antiwar movement of wanting to "cut and run" and pretend that they care more for the interests of the Iraqis—whereas most of them are actually worried about U.S. imperial interests—would be better advised to demand that the United States respect Iraqi sovereignty over Iraqi natural resources and reconstruction. For our part, we believe that there is a moral obligation for the U.S. government to pay reparations to the Iraqi people for all that they have suffered as a consequence of U.S. criminal policies—from the deliberate destruction of Iraq's infrastructure in the 1991 war to the devastation brought by the present invasion and occupation, through the green light given to the Ba'athist regime to crush the mass insurrections of March 1991 and, above all, the murderous embargo inflicted on the Iraqi population from 1991 to 2003.

The withdrawal of U.S. and coalition forces, the end of U.S. economic domination, and the payment of reparations: this is the way to truly serve the principles of justice, as well as the best interests of the people of both Iraq and the United States.

### EVALUATING THE AUTHORS' ARGUMENTS:

In this viewpoint authors Achcar and Shalom recognize that withdrawing American troops from Iraq overnight would cause instability and chaos. Yet they advocate getting all American troops out of Iraq in "the shortest possible timeframe." In your opinion, what is an appropriate timeframe for removing troops from Iraq? Do you think they should be removed at all? If so, at what point in time?

# The United States Should Not Withdraw from Iraq

**Donald Rumsfeld and Peter Pace**

*"Picture Iraq today were we to withdraw and the democratic government to fail and the Zarqawi/ al Qaeda people take over that country. . . . [It] would be a terrible thing."*

In the following viewpoint former secretary of defense Donald Rumsfeld and General Peter Pace testify before Congress on their belief that U.S. forces should not be pulled out of Iraq. Pace states that the Iraqi army, though making progress in training and recruits, is not yet developed enough to take control of the fledgling nation. Furthermore, Rumsfeld warns that pulling U.S. troops out of Iraq would leave the country in chaos, allowing terrorists to swoop down and take control of Iraq. In order to ensure Iraq transitions into a peaceful, democratic nation, Pace and Rumsfeld conclude that American troops must stay in Iraq for the foreseeable future.

Donald Rumsfeld is the former secretary of defense and Peter Pace is a general in the U.S. Army.

Peter Pace, Testimony at Senate Armed Service Committee Hearing on Defense Authorization request for fiscal year 2007. May 17, 2006.

**AS YOU READ, CONSIDER THE FOLLOWING QUESTIONS:**
1. How much does the Iraq War cost U.S. taxpayers per week, as stated by Senator Patrick Leahy?
2. In what way are U.S. troops protecting democracy in Iraq, according to Rumsfeld?
3. How much of Iraq is under control of Iraqi armed forces, according to Pace?

*Sen. Patrick Leahy* (D-VT): I get increasingly worried about [Iraq]—we just seem to have a policy of more of the same. The struggle to form a government goes on interminably. The president says there's a workable strategy in place that will allow for a significant troop withdrawal this year. But since he said that, we've seen a huge rise in ethnic violence, the proliferation of militias that seem out of control, certainly a lengthening of the American casualty roster. Beyond that, it's anybody guess how many Iraqis have been killed or injured.

The American taxpayers get the bill of over a billion dollars a week. The meter is just running on and on. A former senator from Illinois, Senator Dirksen, once said that kind of money adds up. Now we're planning a billion dollar embassy; the most expensive embassy any country has ever built anywhere, and we're planning that. At the same time, we're saying we're not there to control anything, and then we've built bases that are going to be the envy of the military in most countries.

Are we still going to see a significant troop withdrawal this year? . . .

## Iraq Is Not Ready for U.S. Troops to Leave

*Sec. Donald Rumsfeld*: Needless to say, we would hope so, and as the president said, he will wait to receive the recommendations from General Casey and General Abizaid and General Pace as to what they believe the conditions on the ground will permit. And as you continue to go up in Iraqi security forces, both in numbers and equipment and experience, we are being successful in transferring more and more responsibility to them, which, if they get a government, a unity government, and if the government is persuasive to the people of Iraq, that it is—that they should have a stake in its success, then we ought to be able to make reductions.

*Sen. Patrick Leahy:* Let me ask you this— . . . We have spent billions of dollars. We have rosy scenarios all the time. Is there any significant section of Iraq that the Iraqis can control law and order with civil government, with necessary services without U.S. involvement?

*Gen. Peter Pace:* Sir, there are 14 of the 18 provinces right now that are essentially calm, secure—

*Sen. Patrick Leahy:* So we can withdraw from those 14?

*Gen. Peter Pace:* To complete my answer to your question, sir, we are still in the process of assisting in their armed forces and getting these skills they need. We have the battalions coming on line. As I mentioned, 120 are being built; 65 in the lead. There are still the logis-

*Donald Rumsfeld supported keeping U.S. troops in Iraq to prevent terrorists from taking control during the transition.*

tics and command-and-control parts of their army that need to be built for them to be able to sustain themselves completely. So in those areas where they are currently in the lead on the ground, we are assisting them with logistics and command and control, and over time we are building that capacity for them as well.

*Sen. Patrick Leahy*: General, in those 14, are there any one of them that the U.S. forces can withdraw completely in the next three months?

*Gen. Peter Pace*: No, sir. . . .

## Troop Withdrawal Would Increase Terrorism

*Sec. Donald Rumsfeld*: I think one way to look at the first part of your question is to picture Iraq today were we to withdraw and the democratic government to fail and the Zarqawi/al Qaeda people take over that country and turn it into the kind of safe haven that they had in Afghanistan. These are the people who behead people. These are the people that are funding terrorist attacks in other countries. These are the people who would take that country, and therefore that part of the world, back to the Dark Ages. They want to reestablish a caliphate [an Islamic leadership]. And the dire consequences for the people of Iraq, the 25 million people, that 12 million of them went out and voted for their constitution and their democratic election. It is a country that's big, it's important. It has oil, it has water, it has history. And for it to be turned over to extremists would be a terrible thing for that part of the world, and for the free world, and for free people everywhere, in my view. . . .

## Working Toward Troop Withdrawal

*Sen. Richard Durbin* (D-IL): Mr. Secretary, I've reviewed your testimony before this subcommittee since the invasion of Iraq, and it has been consistent. It consistently tells us the Iraqi forces are better than ever; the time is coming very soon when they will be ready to stand and fight for their own country; and yet, as the years have gone by, despite your testimony, we still have 135,000 or more American soldiers with their lives on the line. We've lost 2,450 of our best and bravest. Over 20,000 have suffered serious life-changing injuries and come home, and our Senate has spoken—that this is to be a year of significant transition.

# The Mounting Costs of the Iraq War

As of 2005, the U.S. had spent an estimated **$204.4 billion** fighting the war in Iraq.

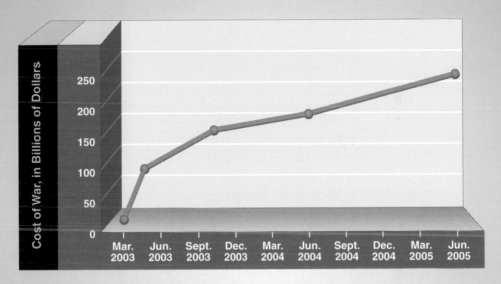

What $204.4 billion could have paid for in the U.S. for one year:
Affordable housing units: **1.8 million** or
Scholarships for university students: **40 million** or
Head Start slots for a year: **27 million**

What $204.4 billion could have paid for around the globe for three years:
Full funding for global anti-hunger efforts **and**
Full funding of worldwide AIDS programs **and**
Full funding for every child in the world for basic immunizations

**Estimated cost of war to date to every U.S. citizen: $727**

Source: Institute for Policy Studies and Foreign Policy In Focus. By Phyllis Bennis, Erik Leaver, and the IPS Iraq Task Force; a comprehensive accounting of the costs of the war on the United States, Iraq, and the World. Report released August 31st, 2005.

I have heard nothing in your testimony, as I've listened to it—it's been related to me—to suggest that you have plans to make this a year for significant transition in Iraq. Can you tell us that before the end of this calendar year, a significant number of American troops will be redeployed, out of harm's way in Iraq?

*Sec. Donald Rumsfeld*: No. No one can. It's obviously our desire and the desire of the troops and the desire of the Iraqi people. No one wants foreign forces in their country.

The president has the—is the one who will make the decision in the executive branch of the government. He has said that he's responsive to General Abizaid and General Casey and General Pace's recommendations and that their recommendations are going to be based on conditions on the ground.

We've gone from a high of 160,000. Today we're at about 133,000, I think. We have every hope that we'll be able to continue making reductions as the Iraqi security forces continue to take over responsibility, as General Pace has described they're currently doing. . . .

## Turning Power Over to Iraqis

*Sen. Richard Durbin*: Well, when we talk about significant transition, I'm afraid I don't have any evidence of it yet, in terms of—

*Sec. Donald Rumsfeld*: There's been one transition, Senator Durbin. And maybe you wouldn't characterize it that way, but clearly there's been a shift in weight within the roles that the coalition forces are playing in Iraq, away from patrolling and over towards the training and the equipping and the mentoring and the embedded process within now not just the Ministry of Defense forces but also the Ministry of Interior forces. That's—that is a shift. At least I would characterize it—wouldn't you, General?

*Gen. Peter Pace*: Sir, there's a continuing process here. We started at the beginning of this calendar year with almost 160,000 troops on the ground. We're down to about 133,000, as the secretary pointed out. We went from almost 20 brigades during the turnover and the election security, down to 15 brigades now. . . .

So the Iraqi armed forces are taking over more and more territory. And I can show you a map, when we're done, sir, that shows you, basically in two colors, how much of the country, which is about 25 percent right now, has been—is under the control of Iraqi forces. And about half of Baghdad is in that territory, sir.

*Sen. Richard Durbin:* Thank you, General.

# The United States Should Prevent Iran from Becoming a Nuclear Power

*"The Bush Administration must press the diplomatic case at the [UN] Security Council to isolate Iran."*

**James Phillips and Brett Schaefer**

In 2005 Iran restarted its nuclear program despite the objections of the United States, the International Atomic Energy Agency, and several European nations. In the following viewpoint researchers James Phillips and Brett Schaefer argue that the UN Security Council will not be able to prevent Iran from attaining nuclear weapons technology. Therefore, they believe, the United States must take charge and prevent the rogue nation from becoming nuclear. The most effective way to contain Iran's nuclear program, according to the authors, is to increase sanctions against Iran, spread those sanctions to other U.S. trading partners, and increase the pressure on the UN to isolate Iran. The authors conclude that under no circumstances must the United States allow Iran to acquire nuclear technology.

James Phillips, Web Memo, Washington, DC: Heritage Foundation, 2006. Copyright 2006 The Heritage Foundation. Reproduced by permission.

Phillips and Schaefer are research fellows at the Heritage Foundation, a think tank that makes U.S. policy recommendations.

**AS YOU READ, CONSIDER THE FOLLOWING QUESTIONS:**
1. Why did Iran first stop its nuclear program in 2003, as reported by the authors?
2. According to Phillips and Schaefer, why did Iran believe it was safe to restart the nuclear program in 2005?
3. Why do the authors believe Iran cannot be trusted with nuclear weapons?

After years of diplomatic foot-dragging, procrastination, and wishful thinking, the International Atomic Energy Agency's (IAEA) Board finally is slated to vote [in March 2006] on whether to refer Iran's suspicious nuclear activities to the UN Security Council for possible action. Iran, as usual, is trying to delay a diplomatic confrontation by dividing key nations with empty promises and further negotiation. Its chief nuclear negotiator, Ali Larijani, has even resorted to blackmail: "If we are referred to the Security Council, problems might occur for others as well as us," he said on March 5. "We would not like to use our oil as a weapon. We would not like to make other countries suffer." The United States and its allies must rebuff this ploy and reject any last-minute diplomatic smokescreens that Iran may try to use to derail action by the IAEA. The U.S. should push for a prompt IAEA referral and confront Iran's violations of its commitments under the Nuclear Non-Proliferation Treaty (NPT) in the UN Security Council.

For now, Tehran is flirting with a Russian proposal that would give it access to uranium enrichment facilities in Russia, but it still clings to its demand for the right to enrich uranium on its own soil, which would increase the risk that uranium could be diverted into a nuclear weapons program. That outcome is unacceptable.

## Iran's Attempt to Procure Nuclear Weapons
The current crisis has its roots in the August 2002 discovery of an Iranian uranium enrichment plant at Natanz and a heavy water production

plant at Arak, both of which Iran had hidden for many years, in violation of its NPT obligations.

To avoid referral to the UN Security Council, Iran agreed to suspend its uranium enrichment efforts in October 2003. Tehran undoubtedly was influenced by the successful military campaigns by U.S.-led coalitions that toppled neighboring regimes in Afghanistan in 2001 and Iraq in 2003.

Iran engaged Britain, France, and Germany (the EU3) in diplomatic negotiations and made tactical concessions to defuse the crisis and stave off international sanctions. But Iran never backed away from its stated goal of acquiring a full nuclear fuel cycle, which could be used to produce fuel for nuclear reactors as well as fissile material for nuclear weapons.

## Bold Iranian Moves and Weak European Action

The installation of a new hard-line Iranian government led by President Mahmoud Ahmadinejad in the summer of 2005 led to a more confrontational strategy. The new government, which criticized the diplomatic concessions made by former President Mohammed Khatami, apparently concluded that Iran's diplomatic position had been bolstered by rising oil prices, the cultivation of diplomatic support from Russia and China, and the perception that the U.S. was bogged down in Iraq and so no longer posed an immediate military threat.

In August 2005, Iran resumed converting yellowcake into uranium hexafluoride, a preliminary step before uranium enrichment, at its nuclear facility in Isfahan. It removed IAEA seals from three of its nuclear facilities on January 10, 2006, and announced the resumption of its uranium enrichment activities at Natanz. This ended the partial freeze of its nuclear program, violated scores of IAEA resolutions, and revealed Iran's bad faith in its diplomatic dialogue with the EU3.

# Iran's Nuclear Weapons Program

At least six Iranian cities are believed to contain facilities related to the research and development of nuclear weapons.

## Legend

 **R** Research reactors/ facilities

 Uranium enrichment facility

Uranium mines

 **H** Heavy water facilities

 **U** Uranium processing facility

 **L** Light-water reactor

The IAEA responded with a weak resolution on February 4 that reported Iran's activities to the Security Council. However, Security Council action was delayed until IAEA Director General Mohammed El-Baradei briefed the IAEA Board on March 6 about his official report on Iran's nuclear activities. The IAEA Board now is expected to review the report and vote on referring Iran to the Security Council by the end of this week.

Still, this leaves Iran another opportunity to defuse the crisis and avert concerted international action. It could suddenly reverse course and embrace the Russian proposal in a last-ditch attempt to avert an IAEA referral. Or it could hold fast to its provocative policy, counting on Russia and China to intercede on its behalf in the Security Council.

## Iran Wants World Conflict

President Ahmadinejad is a true believer in [former Iranian leader Ayatollah] Khomeini's 1979 revolution and is inclined to confrontation. Unlike his predecessor, President Khatami, who advocated a "Dialogue of Civilizations," Ahmadinejad advocates a clash of civilizations, with Iran leading the Islamic world against the United States and Israel.

Ahmadinejad will likely continue his defiant rejection of demands that Iran abandon its nuclear ambitions. Already he has ordered "full scale enrichment" of uranium and ended Iranian cooperation with surprise inspections under the additional protocol of the NPT. Moreover, Ahmadinejad has threatened to withdraw from the NPT altogether.

But cooler heads may yet prevail. Former President Rafsanjani, whom Ahmadinejad defeated in last year's elections, has called for prudence and may be able to convince others. Ayatollah Khamenei, Iran's Supreme Guide, is the ultimate arbiter of Iran's foreign policy and may seek to sidestep international sanctions with easily revocable diplomatic promises.

But Iran appears willing to take its chances in the Security Council. Tehran calculates that Russia and China, both of which have aided Iran's civilian nuclear program and sold it weapons, have a vested economic and strategic interest in maintaining good relations with Iran.

In the past, Russia and China have acted as Iran's protectors, and they could use their influence and the threat of a veto to delay, dilute, or block effective sanctions in the Security Council.

## The United States Must Prevent Iran from Becoming Nuclear

If Russia and China continue to shield Iran, the best that can be expected from the Security Council is a symbolic slap on the wrist through limited diplomatic or economic sanctions. The U.S. therefore must make contingency plans to work with Britain, France, Germany, the EU, Japan, and other interested nations to impose targeted economic sanctions outside the UN framework.

The U.S. already has strong unilateral sanctions in place, but it can tighten them still further. For instance, it could ban the importation

*Many nations fear the impact of weapons that could be developed by Iran if they are allowed to continue their nuclear program.*

of Iranian pistachios and oriental rugs, both of which were exempted from sanctions by the Clinton Administration in a failed effort to launch a diplomatic dialogue with Tehran. The U.S should also rigorously enforce the Iran-Libya Sanctions Act, which penalizes non-Iranian companies that invest in Iran's oil industry.

Despite the UN's weakness in confronting Iran, the Bush Administration must press the diplomatic case at the Security Council to isolate Iran and set the stage for further sanctions, increased international cooperation in containing Iran, and possible military action as a last resort.

## EVALUATING THE AUTHORS' ARGUMENTS:

In this viewpoint the authors argue that because the UN Security Council will be unable to control Iran's nuclear ambitions, the United States must do it. What do you think? Do you believe it is the job of the United States to monitor and control Iran's nuclear program? Would it be worth going to war over? Why or why not? Cite evidence from the texts you have read.

# The United States Should Not Worry About the Threat from Iran

**Charley Reese**

*"Iran isn't going to attack anybody. It hasn't attacked anyone in the past 100 years."*

In the following viewpoint author Charley Reese challenges the claim that Iran is a threat to the United States. Iran has not attacked anyone in more than one hundred years, points out Reese, and there is no reason to believe it will start anytime soon. Furthermore, even if it did want nuclear weapons, Iran is many years away from having the capability to produce them. Misinformation about Iran has distorted public opinion about its intentions, and Reese concludes that Iran does not constitute a threat to the United States.

Reese is a syndicated columnist who writes about a multitude of social and political issues.

Charley Reese, "No War with Iran," King Features Syndicate, June 2, 2006, Copyright American Educational Trust Aug 2006. © King Features Syndicate. Reprinted with Special Permission of North America Syndicate.

I f we allow the Bush administration to drag this country into a war with Iran, we should all burn our voter-registration cards and go ahead and admit that we are no longer worthy of being citizens of a self-governing republic. For heaven's sake, the administration is employing the same tactics it used to justify the war against Iraq— refusal to negotiate, lies, disinformation, and demonization of the Iranian leader. Are we going to fall for the exact same con job all over again? If so, we are far too dumb to be trusted near a voting booth.

## Misinformation About Iran

Recently, a story was floated that the Iranians had passed legislation requiring religious minorities to wear an identifying badge. "Nazi, Nazi" cried the neocon warmongers. Trouble is, the story was completely false. No such legislation was passed, and this bit of disinformation was knocked askew by the representative of Iran's Jewish community in the Iranian parliament. The source of the story was an Iranian who had been a big shot when the shah [Iranian king] was in power and is now with a public-relations firm that represents—surprise—many of the neoconservatives.

> **FAST FACT**
>
> Prior to the 1979 Islamic Revolution, Iran was a staunch ally of the United States and was regarded as a guardian of U.S. interests in the Middle East.

Israeli Prime Minister Ehud Olmert also told a big whopper when he said Iran was only months away from making a nuclear bomb. No nuclear expert I'm aware of agrees with that assessment, and Olmert is no nuclear expert. Even assuming Iran wants a bomb, it is years away from being able to produce one.

## Gunning for War

It's clear that the Bush administration has chosen war. One, it refuses to negotiate with Iran; two, it refuses to recognize Iran's right, as a signer of the Nuclear Nonproliferation Treaty, to enrich uranium for peaceful purposes; three, it has already set up an office in the Pentagon and another in the State Department to agitate for regime change; and four, it has begun its anti-Iranian propaganda campaign.

President Bush is a liar when he says he wants to use diplomacy to end the crisis. In the first place, he created the crisis; in the second place, he refuses to negotiate; and in the third place, he has, for all practical purposes, issued an ultimatum: Give up your right to enrich uranium, or we'll attack.

No country in the world wants us to attack Iran except Israel. That's no surprise. If the American people haven't figured out that Israel exerts an undue and injurious influence on the American government, then that's another reason for them to tear up their voter-registration cards.

And if driving toward war with Iran isn't bad enough, the Bush administration has restarted the Cold War with Russia by its incessant criticism of Vladimir Putin's government. I think, sometimes, that the

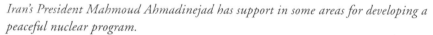

*Iran's President Mahmoud Ahmadinejad has support in some areas for developing a peaceful nuclear program.*

whole Bush administration is out of touch with reality and should be on medication, starting with the president and vice president.

When you consider the wars, the profligate spending, the out-of-control debt and trade deficits, the refusal to control the borders, the alienation of most of the world and the constant spitting on the Constitution and civil liberties, you can conclude that this administration is going to destroy the United States as we know it. I don't say that lightly. I never in a million years would have imagined that this administration would do what it's done.

And if you are one of those armchair jingoists who thinks it's fun to kill foreigners, just keep that thought in mind when you have to pay $10 a gallon for gasoline and the economy comes crashing down on your head. Sure, we can damage Iran's nuclear facilities and kill a lot of Iranians, but we can't do it and keep the oil flowing out of the Persian Gulf at the same time.

## There Is No Threat from Iran

It isn't out of concern for the Iranians that the rest of the world doesn't want a war. It's because other nations recognize the damage it will cause the world economy. It's also because they recognize that this is a phony crisis, like Iraq's mythical weapons of mass destruction.

Even if Iran developed a nuclear weapon, so what. We have thousands; the Israelis have hundreds. Iran isn't going to attack anybody. It hasn't attacked anyone in the past 100 years.

**EVALUATING THE AUTHOR'S ARGUMENT:**

In this viewpoint Reese makes the point that it is not fair to prevent Iran from having weapons when the United States has thousands and other nations have hundreds. What do you think? Is it possible to say which nations should be allowed to have nuclear weapons and which are not? How would you go about deciding which nations should be allowed to have nuclear technology?

# Facts About the Middle East

## Middle East Demographics

The Middle East is a region without precise boundaries. Therefore, definitions of what countries are in the Middle East can change. It is widely agreed that the Middle East includes: Bahrain, Egypt, Iran, Iraq, Israel, Jordan, Kuwait, Lebanon, Oman, Palestinian Territories, Qatar, Saudi Arabia, Sudan, Syria, the United Arab Emirates, and Yemen. Sometimes North African countries such as Libya or Asian countries such as Afghanistan are included.

| Country | Area (Km²) | Population |
|---|---|---|
| Bahrain | 660 | 698,585 |
| Egypt | 1,000,000 | 78,887,007 |
| Iran | 1,650,000 | 68,688,433 |
| Iraq | 434,000 | 26,783,383 |
| Israel | 20,700 | 7,026,000 |
| Jordan | 98,000 | 5,153,378 |
| Kuwait | 17,800 | 2,418,393 |
| Lebanon | 10,452 | 3,874,050 |
| Oman | 212,000 | 3,102,229 |
| Palestinian Territories | 6,275 | 3,889,248 |
| Qatar | 11,437 | 885,359 |
| Saudi Arabia | 2,240,000 | 27,019,731 |
| Sudan | 2,510,000 | 41,236,378 |
| Syria | 185,000 | 18,881,361 |
| United Arab Emirates | 78,000 | 2,602,713 |
| Yemen | 527,970 | 21,456,188 |

- Israel is the Middle East's only Jewish state and only democracy.
- The most common religions found in the Middle East are the Baha'i faith, Christianity, Islam, Judaism, and Zoroastrianism.
- Ethnic groups in the Middle East include Africans, Arabs, Assyrians, Armenians, Azeris, Berbers, Chaldeans, Druze, Greeks, Jews, Kurds, Maronites, Persians, Tajiks, Turks, and Turkmen.
- The main languages spoken are Arabic, Berber, Persian, Turkish, Kurdish, Azeri, Armenian, Assyrian (also known as Aramaic), Syriac, Urdu, and Hebrew.

## Facts About War in the Middle East

The Middle East has been an ongoing scene of political turmoil and major warfare, including:
- World War I (1914–1918)
- World War II (1939–1945)
- The Arab-Israeli Wars, which include:
  - The 1948–1949 War (between the new state of Israel and forces from Egypt, Syria, Transjordan (now called Jordan), Lebanon, and Iraq
  - The 1956 War (between Israel and Egypt)
  - The 1967 War or the Six-Day War (between Israel and Syria, Egypt, and Jordan)
  - The 1973–1974 War or the Yom Kippur War (between Israel and Egypt, Syria, Jordan, and Libya)
  - The 1982 War (between Lebanon and Israel)
  - The 2006 War (between Lebanon and Israel)
  - The first Palestinian intifada (uprising against Israel from 1987 to 1990)
  - The second Palestinian intifada (uprising against Israel from 2000 to present)
- The 1980–1988 Iran-Iraq War
- The Persian Gulf War of 1991 (between the United States and Iraq)
- The 2003 Iraq War (to present)

# Facts About the Middle East and Terrorism

The following groups have been designated by the U.S. State Department as terrorist organizations and are based inside or near the Middle East:

**Organization Name:** Abu Nidal Organization (ANO), also known as Fatah
**Based in:** Iraq
**Targets and Goals:** Targets the United States, UK, France, Israel, moderate Palestinians, the PLO, Arab countries
**Members:** A few hundred
**Active Since:** 1974
**Methods and Activities:** Attacks in twenty countries, killing or injuring nine hundred. Leader Abu Nidal died in 2002

**Organization Name:** Al-Aqsa Martyrs Brigade
**Based in:** West Bank, Gaza Strip, Israel
**Targets and Goals:** To drive Israelis out of region and to establish a Palestinian state
**Members:** Unknown
**Active Since:** 2000
**Methods and Activities:** Shootings, suicide operations (first Palestinian female suicide bombing)

**Organization Name:** Ansar al-Islam (AI)
**Based in:** Iraq
**Targets and Goals:** Aims to create an Islamic state in Iraq; allied with al Qaeda
**Members:** Five hundred to one thousand
**Active Since:** 2001
**Methods and Activities:** Ambushes and attacks

**Organization Name:** Asbat al-Ansar
**Based in:** Lebanon
**Targets and Goals:** Aims to create Islamic state, opposes peace with Israel
**Members:** Three hundred
**Active Since:** 1990s

**Methods and Activities:** Assassinations, bombings of Western targets

**Organization Name:** Gama'a al-Islamiyya
**Based in:** Egypt
**Targets and Goals:** Aims to replace Egypt's government with an Islamic state
**Members:** Unknown
**Active Since:** 1973
**Methods and Activities:** 1993 World Trade Center bombings, attacks on tourists

**Organization Name:** Hamas (Islamic Resistance Movement)
**Based in:** West Bank, Gaza Strip, Israel
**Targets and Goals:** Aims to replace Israel with Palestinian Islamic state using political and violent means
**Members:** Unknown
**Active Since:** 1987
**Methods and Activities:** Large-scale suicide bombings and attacks against Israelis

**Organization Name:** Hizballah (Party of God)
**Based in:** Lebanon, worldwide cells
**Targets and Goals:** Dedicated to eliminating Israel, is anti–United States and anti-Israel
**Members:** Hundreds
**Active Since:** 1982
**Methods and Activities:** Suicide bombings, hijacked 1985 TWA Flight 847; rocket attacks against Israel in 2006

**Organization Name:** Islamic Movement of Uzbekistan (IMU)
**Based in:** South Asia, Tajikistan, Iran
**Targets and Goals:** Aims to establish an Islamic state and fight anti-Islamic opponents
**Members:** Fewer than five hundred
**Active Since:** 1991
**Methods and Activities:** Car bombs, taking foreign hostages, most active in Kyrgyzstan and Tajikistan

**Organization Name:** Al-Jihad (AJ)
**Based in:** Egypt, Yemen, Afghanistan, Pakistan, Lebanon, UK
**Targets and Goals:** Aims to replace the Egyptian government with Islamic state, attack U.S., Israeli interests
**Members:** Hundreds
**Active Since:** 1970s
**Methods and Activities:** Attacks on Egyptian government personnel, assassinated Egyptian president Anwar Sadat

**Organization Name:** Kahane Chai (Kach)
**Based in:** Israel, West Bank
**Targets and Goals:** Organizes protests against the Israeli government
**Members:** Unknown
**Active Since:** 1994
**Methods and Activities:** Threats made to Arabs, Palestinians, and Israeli officials

**Organization Name:** Kongra-Gel (KGK), also known as Kurdistan Workers' Party (PKK)
**Based in:** Turkey, Middle East
**Targets and Goals:** Targets Turkish security forces, officials, and villagers who oppose organization
**Members:** Four thousand to five thousand
**Active Since:** 1974
**Methods and Activities:** Attack diplomatic and commercial facilities, bomb tourist sites

**Organization Name:** Mujahedin-e Khalq Organization (MEK)
**Based in:** Iraq
**Targets and Goals:** Largest armed Iranian opposition group advocates a secular Iranian regime
**Members:** Over three thousand
**Active Since:** 1960s
**Methods and Activities:** Assassinations, terrorist bombings, foreign military-aided assaults

**Organization Name:** Palestine Islamic Jihad (PIJ)
**Based in:** Israel, West Bank, Gaza Strip

**Targets and Goals:** Targets Israeli military and civilians, opposes secularism
**Members:** Unknown
**Active Since:** 1970s
**Methods and Activities:** Suicide bombings, attacks on Israeli interests

**Organization Name:** Palestine Liberation Front (PLF)
**Based in:** Iraq
**Targets and Goals:** Known for aerial attacks against Israel
**Members:** Unknown
**Active Since:** 1970s
**Methods and Activities:** Attack on Italian ship *Achille Lauro*, murder of a U.S. citizen

**Organization Name:** Popular Front for the Liberation of Palestine (PFLP)
**Based in:** Syria, Lebanon, Israel, West Bank, Gaza Strip
**Targets and Goals:** Targets Israel's "illegal occupation" of Palestine and opposes negotiations with Israel
**Members:** Unknown
**Active Since:** 1967
**Methods and Activities:** International terrorist acts in the 1970s, attacks against Israel and moderate Arab targets since 1978

**Organization Name:** Popular Front for the Liberation of Palestine— General Command (PFLP-GC)
**Based in:** Syria
**Targets and Goals:** Attacks in Europe and the Middle East. Targets Israel, West Bank, and Gaza Strip
**Members:** Hundreds
**Active Since:** 1968
**Methods and Activities:** Unusual attacks: hot air balloons, hang gliders, Lebanese guerrilla operations

**Organization Name:** Al Qaeda
**Based in:** Southeast Asia, Middle East, worldwide cells
**Targets and Goals:** Targets "non-Islamic" regimes and U.S. citizens

**Members:** Several thousand
**Active Since:** 1980s
**Methods and Activities:** Bombings of embassies and USS *Cole;* September 11, 2001, U.S. attacks

**Organization Name:** Al Qaeda in Iraq
**Based in:** Iraq
**Targets and Goals:** Targets U.S. soldiers and Iraqi citizens; leader Abu Musab al-Zarqawi killed by U.S. in 2006
**Members:** One thousand
**Active Since:** 2003
**Methods and Activities:** Major and numerous terrorist attacks in Iraq

**Organization Name:** Tanzim Qa'idat al-Jihad fi Bilad al-Rafidayn (QJBR) also known as Al-Zarqawi Network and al Qaeda in Iraq
**Based in:** Iraq
**Targets and Goals:** Aims to expel coalition forces and establish Islamic state in Iraq, then move to Syria, Lebanon, Israel, and Jordan
**Members:** Unknown
**Active Since:** 2003
**Methods and Activities:** Many bombings, killing hundreds; assassination of key Iraqi political figures; beheadings of Americans

# Glossary

**Al-Aqsa intifada:** The Palestinian uprising, sometimes called the second intifada, which began in September 2000 when former Israeli prime minister Ariel Sharon made a controversial visit to the Al-Aqsa Mosque in East Jerusalem. The intifada has been characterized by violence and terrorism against Israeli civilians.

**Al-Aqsa Mosque:** Third holiest shrine in the Muslim world. Located on the Haram al-Sharif in Jerusalem.

**anti-Semitism:** Hostility and discrimination toward Jews.

**Baghdad:** Capital city of Iraq.

**Beirut:** Capital city of Lebanon.

**Camp David Accords of 1978:** The 1978 agreement between Israel and Egypt that led to a peace treaty between the two nations. It was the first peace treaty between the Jewish state and any of its Arab neighbors.

**Dome of the Rock:** The mosque erected in the seventh century on the spot where Muhammad ascended to heaven during his Night Journey to Jerusalem. The Rock also refers to the spot where Abraham prepared to sacrifice his son Isaac. The Dome is also built on the site of the Jewish Temple and thus can be a source of tension between Jews and Muslims.

**Druze:** Members of a religious sect that broke with Islam nearly a thousand years ago. Members live mostly in Lebanon and Syria and in the mountains around Israel.

**Fatah:** The Palestinian National Liberation Movement, the largest group in the PLO. Though Fatah was once primarily known as a guerilla terrorist group, it has evolved into a legitimate political movement.

**Gaza Strip:** The rectangular region on the coast of the Mediterranean Sea between Israel and Egypt. It has a population of more than a million Palestinians and about seven thousand Israeli settlers.

**Hamas:** The Islamic Resistance Movement, tied to the Muslim Brotherhood, calling for the creation of an Islamic state in all of historic

Palestine. Hamas has a military wing that conducts terrorist acts on Israeli civilians and a political wing that was elected to power in January 2006.

**intifada:** "Shaking off" in Arabic. The first intifada took place in the Occupied Territories from 1987–1993 and a second one began in September 2000. The goal of both intifadas has been to end Israeli control of the territories.

**Islamic Jihad:** A Palestinian resistance organization whose members seek to create an Islamic state in all of historic Palestine. Like Hamas, they use terrorism and suicide bombers to achieve their goal.

**Judea and Samaria:** The Biblical names for the eastern part of Palestine that others refer to as the West Bank.

**Koran or Qur'an:** The Holy Book of Islam, the word of God as received by Muhammad.

**Occupied Territories:** The Gaza Strip and the West Bank, including East Jerusalem, occupied by Israel since 1967.

**Palestinian Authority (PA):** The Palestinian governing body that has limited authority over the West Bank and Gaza Strip.

**Partition Plan:** The plan devised by the United Nations in 1947 to carve the area of Palestine into both a Jewish and an Arab state.

**Quartet:** Refers to four parties, the European Union, the United Nations, the United States, and Russia, who have sponsored a "Roadmap for Peace" to end the Israeli-Palestinian conflict.

**Ramallah:** Palestinian city north of Jerusalem; headquarters of the Palestinian Authority.

**right of return:** An individual right granted all Palestinian refugees in UN Resolution 194. Whether the Palestinians have this right is contested by most Israelis, and therefore this issue remains one of the most difficult issues in achieving a permanent peace between the two parties.

**Roadmap for Peace:** A plan embraced by the Quartet for the resolution of the Israeli-Palestinian conflict.

**Shiite Muslims:** Members of the second-largest branch of Islam. Shiites believe that Ali, Muhammad's direct descendant, was his only rightful successor. Shiites make up the majority in Iran and Iraq but are a minority in many other Muslim countries.

**Sunni Muslims:** Members of the largest branch of Islam in the Middle East; Sunni sects are orthodox, believing that the first four caliphs were Muhammad's rightful successors.

**Tehran:** Capital city of Iran.

**West Bank:** Large territory between the Jordan River and Israel's 1949 border. It contains the parts of Jerusalem east of the 1948–1949 armistice line. Jordan annexed the West Bank after the 1948 war; the West Bank has been occupied by Israel since 1967.

# Organizations to Contact

The editors have compiled the following list of organizations concerned with the issues debated in this book. The descriptions are derived from materials provided by the organizations. All have publications or information available for interested readers. The list was compiled on the date of publication of the present volume; the information provided here may change. Be aware that many organizations take several weeks or longer to respond to inquiries, so allow as much time as possible.

**American Enterprise Institute (AEI)**
1150 Seventeenth St. NW
Washington, DC 20036
(202) 862-5800
fax: (202) 862-7177
Web site: www.aei.org

The American Enterprise Institute for Public Policy Research is a scholarly research institute that is dedicated to preserving limited government, private enterprise, and a strong foreign policy and national defense. It publishes books, including *Democratic Realism: An American Foreign Policy for a Unipolar World;* and *The Islamic Paradox: Shiite Clerics, Sunni Fundamentalists, and the Coming of Arab Democracy;* and a bimonthly magazine, *American Enterprise.*

**American Jewish Committee (AJC)**
PO Box 705
New York, NY 10150
(212) 751-4000
fax: (212) 838-2120
e-mail: PR@ajc.org
Web site: www.ajc.org

AJC works to strengthen U.S.-Israeli relations, build international support for Israel, and support the Israeli-Arab peace process. The committee's numerous publications include the *AJC Journal,* the report

*Muslim Anti-Semitism: A Clear and Present Danger,* and the papers "Iran and the Palestinian War Against Israel" and "The Arab Campaign to Destroy Israel."

### Americans for Middle East Understanding (AMEU)
475 Riverside Dr., Rm. 245
New York, NY 10115-0245
(212) 870-2053
fax: (212) 870-2050
e-mail: info@ameu.org
Web site: www.ameu.org

AMEU's purpose is to foster a better understanding in America of the history, goals, and values of Middle Eastern cultures and peoples, the rights of Palestinians, and the forces shaping U.S. policy in the Middle East. AMEU publishes the *Link*, a bimonthly newsletter, as well as books and pamphlets on the Middle East.

### AMIDEAST
1730 M St. NW, Suite 1100
Washington, DC 20036-4505
(202) 776-9600
fax: (202) 776-7000
e-mail: inquiries@amideast.org
Web site: www.amideast.org

AMIDEAST promotes understanding and cooperation between Americans and the people of the Middle East and North Africa through education and development programs. It publishes a number of books for all age groups, including *Islam: A Primer.*

### Arab World and Islamic Resources and School Services (AWAIR)
2137 Rose St.
Berkeley, CA 94709
(510) 704-0517
e-mail: awair@igc.apc.org
Web site: www.telegraphave.com/gui/awairproductinfo.html

AWAIR provides materials and services for educators teaching about Arabs and Islam for precollege-level educators. It publishes many books and videos, including *The Arab World Studies Notebook*, *Middle Eastern Muslim Women Speak*, and *Islam*.

## The Brookings Institution
1775 Massachusetts Ave. NW
Washington, DC 20036
(202) 797-6000
fax: (202) 797-6004
e-mail: brookinfo@brook.edu
Web site: www.brookings.org

The institution, founded in 1927, is a think tank that conducts research and education in foreign policy, economics, government, and the social sciences. In 2001 it began America's Response to Terrorism, a project that provides briefings and analysis to the public and which is featured on the center's Web site. It publishes the quarterly *Brookings Review*, periodic *Policy Briefs*, and books on the Middle East including *Crescent of Crisis* and *Iran, Islam, and Democracy*.

## Cato Institute
1000 Massachusetts Ave. NW
Washington, DC 20001-5403
(202) 842-0200
fax: (202) 842-3490
e-mail: cato@cato.org
Web site: www.cato.org

The institute is a nonpartisan public policy research foundation dedicated to limiting the role of government and protecting individual liberties. It publishes the quarterly magazine *Regulation*, the bimonthly *Cato Policy Report*, and numerous policy papers and articles.

## Center for Middle Eastern Studies
University of Texas
Austin, TX 78712
(512) 471-3881
fax: (512) 471-7834
e-mail: cmes@menic.texas.edu
Web site: http://menic.utexas.edu/menic/cmes

The center was established by the U.S. Department of Education to promote a better understanding of the Middle East. It provides research and instructional materials and publishes three series of books on the Middle East: the Modern Middle East Series, the Middle East Monograph Series, and the Modern Middle East Literatures in Translation Series.

## Council on Foreign Relations
58 E. Sixty-eighth St.
New York, NY 10021
(212) 434-9400
fax: (212) 434-9800
e-mail: communications@cfr.org
Web site: www.cfr.org

The council researches the international aspects of American economic and political policies. Its journal *Foreign Affairs*, published five times a year, provides analysis on global conflicts. Publications include "Threats to Democracy: Prevention and Response" and various articles. A video recording of the proceedings of a December 2005 conference, called "Democracy in the Arab World—Why and How," can be viewed on its Web site.

## Foundation for Middle East Peace
1763 N St. NW
Washington, DC 20036
(202) 835-3650
fax: (202) 835-3651
e-mail: info@fmep.org
Web site: www.fmep.org

The foundation assists the peaceful resolution of the Israeli-Palestinian conflict by making financial grants available within the Arab and Jewish communities. It publishes the bimonthly *Report on Israeli Settlements in the Occupied Territories* and additional books and papers.

## Institute for Palestine Studies (IPS)
3501 M St. NW
Washington, DC 20007
(202) 342-3990

fax: (202) 342-3927
e-mail: ips@ipsjps.org
Web site: www.ipsjps.org

The Institute for Palestine Studies is a private, nonprofit pro-Arab institute unaffiliated with any political organization or government. Established in 1963 in Beirut, the institute promotes research, analysis, and documentation of the Arab-Israeli conflict and its resolution. IPS publishes quarterlies in three languages and maintains offices all over the world. In addition to editing the *Journal of Palestine Studies*, the institute's U.S. branch publishes books and documents on the Arab-Israeli conflict and Palestinian affairs.

**International Institute of Islamic Thought (IIIT)**
PO Box 669
Herndon, VA 20172
(703) 471-1133
fax: (703) 471-3922
e-mail: iiit@iiit.org
Web site: www.iiit.org

This nonprofit academic research facility promotes and coordinates research and related activities in Islamic philosophy, the humanities, and social sciences. It publishes numerous books in both Arabic and English as well as the quarterly *American Journal of Islamic Social Science* and the *Muslim World Book Review*.

**Islamic Supreme Council of America (ISCA)**
1400 Sixteenth St. NW, Rm. B112
Washington, DC 20036
(202) 939-3400
fax: (202) 939-3410
e-mail: staff@islamicsupremecouncil.org
Web site: www.islamicsupremecouncil.org

The ISCA is a nongovernmental religious organization that promotes Islam in America both by providing practical solutions to American Muslims in integrating Islamic teachings with American culture and by teaching non-Muslims that Islam is a religion of moderation, peace, and tolerance. It strongly condemns Islamic extremists and all forms of terrorism. Its Web site includes statements, commentaries, and reports on terrorism, including *Usama bin Laden: A Legend Gone Wrong* and *Jihad: A Misunderstood Concept from Islam.*

### Jordan Information Bureau
2319 Wyoming Ave. NW
Washington, DC 20008
(202) 265-1606
fax: (202) 667-0777
e-mail: jordaninfo@aol.com
Web site: www.jordanembassyus.org/new/jib/indexjib.shtml

The bureau provides political, cultural, and economic information on Jordan. It publishes fact sheets, speeches by Jordanian officials, and government documents, many of which are available on its Web site.

### Middle East Forum
1500 Walnut St., Suite 1050
Philadelphia, PA 19102
(215) 546-5406
fax: (215) 546-5409
e-mail: info@meforum.org
Web site: www.meforum.org

The Middle East Forum is a think tank that works to define and promote American interests in the Middle East. It supports strong American ties with Israel, Turkey, and other democracies as they emerge. It publishes the *Middle East Quarterly*, a policy-oriented journal. Its Web site includes articles, summaries of activities, and a discussion forum.

### Middle East Media Research Institute (MEMRI)
PO Box 27837
Washington, DC 20038-7837
(202) 955-9070
fax: (202) 955-9077
e-mail: memri@erols.com
Web Site: www.memri.org

MEMRI translates and disseminates articles and commentaries from Middle Eastern media sources and provides original research and analysis on the region. Its Jihad and Terrorism Studies Project monitors radical Islamist groups and individuals and their reactions to acts of terrorism around the world.

**Middle East Policy Council (MEPC)**
1730 M St. NW, Suite 512
Washington, DC 20036
(202) 296-6767
fax: (202) 296-5791
e-mail: info@mepc.org
Web site: www.mepc.org

The purpose of this nonprofit organization is to contribute to an understanding of current issues in U.S. relations with countries of the Middle East. It publishes the quarterly journal *Middle East Policy* as well as special reports and books.

**Middle East Research and Information Project (MERIP)**
1500 Massachusetts Ave. NW
Washington, DC 20005
(202) 223-3677
fax: (202) 223-3604
Web site: www.merip.org

MERIP is a nonprofit nongovernmental organization with no links to any religious, educational, or political organizations in the United States or elsewhere. Its mission is to educate the public about the contemporary Middle East with particular emphasis on U.S. foreign policy, human rights, and social justice issues. It publishes the bimonthly *Middle East Report.*

**Middle East Studies Association**
University of Arizona
1643 E. Helen St.
Tucson, AZ 85721
(520) 621-5850
fax: (520) 626-9095
e-mail: mesana@u.arizona.edu
Web site: http://w3fp.arizona.edu/mesassoc

This professional academic association of scholars on the Middle East focuses particularly on the rise of Islam. It publishes the quarterly *International Journal of Middle East Studies* and runs a project for the evaluation of textbooks for coverage of the Middle East.

## The National Endowment for Democracy (NED)
1101 Fifteenth St. NW, Suite 700
Washington, DC 20005
(202) 293-9072
fax: (202) 223-6042
e-mail: info@ned.org

The National Endowment for Democracy (NED) is a private nonprofit organization created in 1983 to strengthen democratic institutions around the world through nongovernmental efforts. It publishes the bimonthly periodical *Journal of Democracy*.

## United Association for Studies and Research
PO Box 1210
Annandale, VA 22003-1210
(703) 750-9011
fax: (703) 750-9010
e-mail: uasr@aol.com
Web site: www.uasr4islam.com

This nonprofit organization examines the causes of conflict in the Middle East and North Africa, the political trends that shape the region's future, and the relationship of the region to more technologically advanced nations. It publishes Islam Under Siege and The Middle East: Politics and Development, two series of occasional papers on current topics.

## United Nations Development Programme (UNDP)
1 United Nations Plaza
New York, NY 10017
(212) 906-5317
Web site: www.undp.org

The United Nations was established in 1945 to, among other things, help nations cooperate in solving international economic, social, cultural, and humanitarian problems. The UNDP engages in global advocacy and analysis to generate knowledge about—and develop policies to—aid developing nations. UNDP's primary areas of interest are democratic governance, poverty reduction, environmental protection, sustainable energy, gender issues, HIV/AIDS, information and communication technology, and crisis prevention and recovery. Numerous reports and facts sheets on these topics are available on the UNDP Web site.

## Washington Institute for Near East Policy
1828 L St. NW
Washington, DC 20036
(202) 452-0650
fax: (202) 223-5364
e mail: info@washingtoninstitute.org
Web site: www.washingtoninstitute.org

The institute is an independent nonprofit research organization that provides information and analysis on the Middle East and U.S. policy in the region. It publishes numerous books, periodic monographs, and reports on regional politics, security, and economics, including *Hezbollah's Vision of the West; Hamas: The Fundamentalist Challenge to the PLO; Democracy and Arab Political Culture,* and *Democracy in the Middle East: Defining the Challenge.*

## Women's Alliance for a Democratic Iraq (WAFDI)
e-mail: sarbaghsalih@cs.com
Web site: www.wafdi.org

The Women's Alliance for a Democratic Iraq (WAFDI) is an international nonpartisan and not-for-profit women's rights organization. WAFDI is dedicated to a free and democratic Iraq with full and equal individual rights for women. The organization is committed to the advancement and empowerment of women in all areas of society, including but not limited to family, economics, education, health, arts, literature, sports, and politics.

# For Further Reading

## Books

Bourke, Edmund, and David N. Yaghoubi, eds. *Struggle and Survival in the Modern Middle East.* Berkeley and Los Angeles, CA: University of California Press, 2006. A fascinating depiction of the lives of ordinary Middle Eastern men and women, peasants, villagers, pastoralists, and urbanites.

Chamberlin, Ann. *History of Women's Seclusion in the Middle East: The Veil in the Looking Glass.* Binghamton, NY: Haworth, 2006. An examination of the practice of seclusion of women throughout the Middle East.

Cleveland, William L. *A History of the Modern Middle East.* Boulder, CO: Westview, 2004. A brief but thorough introduction to the history of this volatile part of the world.

Crotty, William, ed. *Democratic Development and Political Terrorism: The Global Perspective.* Boston: Northeastern University Press, 2005. This collection of original essays examines the global link between democratic development and political terrorism, delving into the uncertainties of dealing with terrorism on an international scale.

Diamond, Larry, Marc F. Plattner, and Daniel Brumberg, eds. *Islam and Democracy in the Middle East.* Baltimore: Johns Hopkins University Press, 2003. Provides a comprehensive assessment of Middle East autocracies and the struggles of state reformers and opposition forces to promote civil liberties, competitive elections, and a pluralistic vision of Islam.

Fuller, Graham E. *The Future of Political Islam.* New York: Palgrave Macmillan, 2004. A broad survey of Islamic political movements.

Galbraith, Peter W. *The End of Iraq: How American Incompetence Created a War Without End.* New York: Simon & Schuster, 2006. A clear-eyed and persuasive case against the Bush administration's nation-building project in Iraq.

Gelvin, James L. *The Modern Middle East: A History.* New York: Oxford

University Press, 2004. A thorough examination of the events that led to the creation of the contemporary Middle East.

Gerner, Deborah J., and Jillian Schwedler, eds. *Understanding the Contemporary Middle East.* Boulder, CO: Lynne Rienner, 2003. An interdisciplinary book that provides an excellent introduction to issues surrounding conflict in the Middle East.

Held, Colbert C. *Middle East Patterns: Places, Peoples, and Politics.* Boulder, CO: Westview, 2005. Contains information on a wide range of issues relating to the Middle East, from soils and climate to religion and government.

Hiro, Dilip. *The Essential Middle East: A Comprehensive Guide.* New York: Carroll & Graf, 2003. An easy-to-read must-have reference for anyone interested in understanding more about the Middle East, written by an expert on the subject.

Lewis, Bernard. *The Crisis of Islam: Holy War and Unholy Terror.* New York: Random House, 2004. Explores the roots of Islamic fundamentalism.

Miller, Debra A. *U.S. Involvement in the Middle East: Inciting Conflict.* San Diego: Lucent, 2004. Explores America's role in fomenting conflict in the region.

Qumsiyeh, Mazin B. *Sharing the Land of Canaan: Human Rights and the Israeli-Palestinian Struggle.* London: Pluto, 2004.

Ricks, Thomas E. *Fiasco: The American Military Adventure in Iraq.* New York: Penguin, 2006. A thorough and devastating history of the war in Iraq from the planning stages through the continued insurgency in early 2006.

Yancey, Diane. *The Middle East: An Overview.* San Diego: Lucent, 2004. Explores many of the causes of conflict in the Middle East, including religious diversity, unresponsive leadership, disputes over land and resources, interference from outside sources, and terrorist groups.

Wasserstein, Bernard. *Israelis and Palestinians: Why Do They Fight? Can They Stop?* New Haven, CT: Yale University Press, 2004. Discusses the issues at hand in the Israeli-Palestinian conflict.

## Periodicals
Basham, Patrick. "Can Iraq Be Democratic?" *Policy Analysis,* January 5, 2004.

Black, Edwin. "Given Its History, Can We Succeed in Iraq?" *History News Network*, December 27, 2004.

Brown, Nathan J. "Living with Palestinian Democracy," *Carnegie Endowment for International Peace, Policy Brief no. 46*, June 2006.

Buchanan, Patrick J. "On Talking with Terrorists," syndicated column, *Creator's Syndicate*, August 5, 2006.

Democracy Now.org. "Ret. Army General William Odom: U.S. Should 'Cut and Run' from Iraq," October 4, 2005. www.democracynow.org.

Finkel, David. "Beyond Iraq: The Spreading Crisis," *Against the Current*, vol. 21, no. 2, May/June 2006.

Fisher, Franklin M., and Annette Huber-Lee. "Economics, Water Management, and Conflict Resolution in the Middle East and Beyond," *Environment*, vol. 48, no. 3, April 2006.

Gardiner, Nile, and James Phillips. "Congress Should Withhold Funds from the UN Relief and Works Agency for Palestine Refugees (UNRWA)," WebMemo #987, Heritage Foundation, February 6, 2006. www.heritage.org.

Glazov, Jamie. "Symposium: The War for the Soul of Iraq," *FrontPageMagazine.com*, December 2, 2005.

———. "Terror in the Skies," *FrontPageMagazine.com*, September 18, 2006. www.frontpage.com.

Halpern, Micah. "Nice Guys Can't Negotiate with Terrorists," *Micah Report*, June 7, 2005.

Hanson, Victor Davis. "Why We Must Stay in Iraq," *Washington Post*, September 4, 2005.

Ignatieff, Michael. "Who Are Americans to Think That Freedom Is Theirs to Spread?" *New York Times Magazine*, June 26, 2005.

Katz, Marisa. "Democratease—Rhetoric v. Reality," *New Republic*, June 6, 2005.

Marshall, Rachelle. "The Real Reason for Israel's Wars on Gaza and Lebanon," *Washington Report on Middle East Affairs*," vol. 25, no. 7.

Moravchik, Joshua. "Among Arab Reformers," *Commentary*, vol. 120, no. 2, September 2005.

Mozah, Sheikha. "Give Arab Women Their Due," *Peninsula*, March 4, 2006. www.thepeninsulaqatar.com.

Nasr, Vali. "The Rise of Muslim Democracy," *Journal of Democracy*, vol. 16, no. 2, April 2005.

O'Sullivan, John. "Hamas Win Isn't Loss for U.S. Policy," *Chicago Sun-Times*, January 31, 2006.

Phillips, James. "Hamas's Victory: The United States Should Not Recognize or Aid a Terrorist Regime," WebMemo #971, Heritage Foundation, January 27, 2006. www.heritage.org.

*Socialist Worker.* "There Can Be No Peace Without Justice," March 15, 2002.

Stauffer, Thomas R. "Turkish, Syrian Water Projects Well on the Way to Squeezing Iraq Dry," *Washington Report on Middle East Affairs*, vol. 23, no. 4, May 2004.

United Nations Development Programme. *Arab Human Development Report*, 2004.

*Wall Street Journal.* "Democracy Angst: What's the Alternative to Promoting Democracy in the Middle East?" editorial, February 27, 2006.

Will, George F. "Can We Make Iraq Democratic?" *City Journal*, Winter 2004.

Zoubiane, Roula. "Water Conflict in the Middle East: The Lebanese-Israeli Case," *International Peace Update*, Summer 2006.

## Web Sites

**Bitterlemons.org** (www.bitterlemons.org). This Web site presents Israeli and Palestinian viewpoints on the Palestinian-Israeli conflict and peace process as well as related regional issues of concern.

**Ha'Aretz Online** (www.haaretzdaily.com). This is an online edition of one of the leading Israeli newspapers published in English.

**Islamic Republic News Agency** (www.irna.com/en). This agency of the government of Iran provides links to news articles and current affairs about that nation and the Middle East.

**Al Jazeera** (www.aljazeera.com). An independent news magazine based in the United Arab Emirates. Contains news and commentary about a wide variety of Middle Eastern affairs.

**MidEastWeb** (www.mideastweb.org). MidEastWeb is a Web site founded by people from different nations who are active in peace education efforts. It features articles and opinions about events in the region, as well as maps and a history of the conflict in the Middle East.

**Palestinian National Authority** (www.pna.gov.ps). The official Web site of the Palestinian National Authority, the organization in charge of Palestinian-administered areas of the West Bank and Gaza Strip.

**Saudi Arabia Ministry of Information** (www.saudinf.com). This official Saudi government site has links to thousands of pages of information on the kingdom of Saudi Arabia.

# Index

# Picture Credits

Cover: © Georgina Bowater/CORBIS

AP Images, 10, 13, 19, 26, 33, 38, 43, 46, 56, 62, 70, 73, 77, 81, 87, 93, 103, 107

Steve Zmina, 15, 21, 27, 31, 40, 49, 53, 64, 89, 95, 101